What others are saying about *Legacy Living*...

"*Legacy Living is an insightful roadmap for crafting a purposeful legacy that goes beyond the self, offering essential steps to utilize personal talents, time, and resources for the betterment of future generations. As a mental health counselor, I wholeheartedly endorse this empowering book, recognizing its potential to inspire individuals to leave a lasting impact, fostering mental well-being through the transformative act of creating a meaningful legacy. Proverbs 13:22."*

Dr. Jada Jackson Hill LMHC, LPC-S
Licensed Professional Counselor - State of Texas
Licensed Mental Health Counselor - State of Florida
Author, Talk Show Host, Life Coach, Communicator
jada@totallifedallas.com

"*I excelled on every level of sports reaching the NBA. I always wanted to leave a mark on the game by having my number retired and winning a championship. After reading this, my perspective on leaving a mark has changed. Leaving a legacy is who you are, not just what people say or hear about you. This is a must read for everyone who wants to make a difference regardless of age, financial status, or location.*"

Micheal Williams
Former NBA Player (Pistons, Timberwolves, Pacers)
Holds NBA Consecutive Free Throw Record
Commercial Construction Business Owner

How to Impact
Future Generations

LEGACY LIVING

Live It, Love It,
Leave It

Tante Williams

Legacy Living
©2024 Tante Williams
All rights reserved.

No part of this book may be reproduced without written permission from the publisher or copyright holder, nor may any part of this book be transmitted in any form or by any means electronic, mechanical, photocopying, recording, or other, without prior written permission from the publisher or copyright holder.

Scriptures taken from the Holy Bible, New International Version©, NIV©. Copyright © 1973, 1978, 1984, 2011 by Biblica, Inc.© Used by permission of Zondervan. All rights reserved worldwide. www.zondervan.com The NIV© and New International Version© are trademarks registered in the United States Patent and Trademark Office by Biblica, Inc.©

Published by: HigherLife Publishing & Marketing
PO Box 623307
Oviedo, FL 32762
(407) 563–4806
www.HigherLifePublishing.com

Cover Design: Amber Weigand-Buckley
Interior Design: Faithe Thomas

ISBN: 979-8-9899401-8-9 paperback
ISBN: 979-8-9899401-9-6 eBook
Library of Congress: 1-13622621231

Printed in the United States of America
10 9 8 7 6 5 4 3 2 1

Contents

<u>8 Parts with Legacies acronym</u>
1. **L**egacies
2. **E**xemplify
3. **G**ive
4. **A**ctivate
5. **C**are
6. **I**nnovate
7. **E**conomics
8. **S**hare

Acknowledgments vii
Intro ix

Part 1: Legacies 1
Chapter 1: Autopilot 3
Chapter 2: Powerful... 9

Part 2: Exemplify...17
Chapter 3: Types of Legacies..19
Chapter 4: A Legacy Leaver: Oseola McCarty of Mississippi 23
Chapter 5: A Legacy Leaving Child: Alex's Lemonade Stand 25
Chapter 6: A Legacy Leaver: Football to Farm 27
Chapter 7: A Legacy Leaver: Lucy Ann Jackson....................29
Chapter 8: A Legacy Leaver: Avi Schiffman........................31
Chapter 9: Weird Legacies & Inheritances 33

Part 3: Give 37
Chapter 10: The Benefits of Giving 39
Chapter 11: Gifts 47

Part 4: Activate 55
Chapter 12: Go 57
Chapter 13: Legacy Placement Assessment 61
Chapter 14: Self-Discovery 71
Chapter 15: Planning 79
Chapter 16: Action 89

Part 5: Care 95
Chapter 17: Motivation 97
Chapter 18: Who to Give To? 103
Chapter 19: Course Correction 113

Part 6: Innovate 119
Chapter 20: Digital Assets 121
Chapter 21: Creative Gifts 125

Part 7: Economics 131
Chapter 22: The Numbers 133
Chapter 23: How to Leave a Financial Gift 139

Part 8: Share 149
Chapter 24: Gather 151
Chapter 25: Share 157
Chapter 26: Give Thanks 159

Acknowledgments

All of my past decisions, experiences, failures, and successes have culminated in this moment today. I am thankful for those who have come into my life for a season and those who have stuck with me since the day we met. I am especially grateful for my husband, Micheal Williams, who has opened my eyes to the true meaning of legacy living.

Intro

You were created to leave a mark on this world. What mark you leave is up to you.

The day you were born, you came out of your mother's womb clothed in purpose, the beginning threads of your legacy. Your purpose clung to you when you uttered your first words; it held on to you when you took your first steps and stuck to you like glue as you toddled through your early years. It didn't matter how easy or difficult your childhood was; your purpose was there, layering your experiences like scaffolding to build you up to reach your legacy.

Why you are here goes hand in hand with what you will leave because wherever your purpose pulls you, your legacy will follow.

My family roots are proudly grounded in heroic determination, historic firsts, and highlights of corporate and athletic success. It is also steeped in alcoholism, drugs, and perversive addictions. I have a choice of which legacy I will continue to carry from my family's lineage, which I will sever from family ties, and which to pass on to my step-children, nieces, nephews, and other youngsters in my community.

My ancestors were brought here to build a powerful land off their backs, creating a civilization that provided only marginal room for people of color. I am here to increase that space in which people of color operate and widen the door of opportunities for future generations of all people.

If you have not thought about what you're leaving this world, it is time to start. The life you are living right now determines the legacy you will leave. Positive legacies don't just happen by accident; they are planned, executed, lived, shaped, communicated, sharpened, experienced, manifested, and polished.

You are never too young or old to start thinking about how you will bless others. As long as you have breath, you have an opportunity to leave a positive mark.

When I ask people to give me an example of a strong legacy, they often speak of President Abraham Lincoln, credited with freeing the slaves, Martin Luther King Jr., who successfully rallied against inequality, or Supreme Court Justice Thurgood Marshall, who successfully argued Brown v. Board of Education. While those legacies are definitely powerful, these popular icons didn't get there without lesser-known legacies building them up.

You don't need to have your name plastered in lights or negotiate some momentous multi-million deal to leave a legacy that can positively impact generations. All you need is a plan and a generous heart to contribute your time, gifts, and resources. The earlier you start on your journey, the more time you have to make an impact. There is no better time than today to start.

In the following pages, you will discover how building out your legacy can elevate your joy and happiness as well as provide a sense of belonging and self-worth. You will see how some legacies were born and how they have improved lives. We will test the strength of your legacy knowledge and provide keys to ensuring your heirs gain a positive gift they can build on generation after generation. You will also lay the foundation for creating your own legacy. If you have already started, there are tools to advance your chosen plan.

Turn the page to open the door to living your legacy life *now*.

Part 1
Legacies

If you're going to live, leave a legacy. Make a mark on the world that can't be erased.

—Maya Angelou, *American poet*

Chapter 1:
Autopilot

Many of us allow our family cycles to operate on autopilot. From generation to generation, we flow with the familial current that what happened to our parents happens to us and will probably happen to our children because that's how it's been and how we expect it to be. But if those rotations are unhealthy or need a tune-up, it's up to us to make the change. There is a process to disrupt destructive patterns or behaviors and set a fresh, new course for our future and generations beyond. The keys lie within us. Let's unlock them together.

Before I dive into this legacy journey, I would like to give you a glimpse into who I am, how I intentionally broke family cycles, and why a positive legacy is such a vital mission for me. Growing up in a blended family in Houston, Texas, I looked slightly different than my four siblings. As a mocha-colored African American girl with hazel eyes (inherited from my mother's side of the family), my tightly curled hair (some would call it nappy) did not match anyone else's in my immediate family. Since my mother and father have relaxed curls, I guessed I inherited my locks from my great-great-grandparents who worked the Mississippi lands shipped here from Africa. I got teased throughout my childhood about my "cat eyes" and, of course, my hair. My toenails curled up at the end of the nail and were itty bitty, according to laughing ladies at the nail salon. They looked just like many of my aunts and cousins, who assured me my feet were petite and beautiful.

Like the physical features I inherited from my ancestors, I received tangible and not tangible gifts from my family, too. I have rights to a piece of "heir" property in northern Louisiana that my mother's grandparents bought back in the early 1900s. It's called "heir" property because the land is passed down from generation to generation without a designated owner. Legally, it's owned by the whole family. Everyone from my great-grandparents' lineage, like my grandmother, her nine siblings, and their bloodline, as well as my grandmother's twelve children and their bloodline, have rights to the property.

Soon after my great-grandparents secured the 200–plus acreage, they had to give up the mineral rights. As the story goes, one of my great-uncles got in legal trouble, and the family was forced to give up mineral rights to keep him out of jail and keep their land intact. My maternal grandparents (mostly my grandmother, Ola) raised 12 children on that farmland, and their children produced 44 grandchildren. Now, the descendants and heirs to the property number more than 100. Many hands far and wide around the broad span of the United States touch the Spivey family deed. While the sprawling land is there for any family member to enjoy, making permanent decisions for the plot is impossible. No individual can legally put a permanent home there without fear of it being contested by other family members. And, since no one person is responsible for paying the property taxes, only a few people pick up the bill so the inheritance won't be lost.

Both sets of my grandparents on my mother's and father's sides were Christian and loyal to their church. My grandparents and parents cemented the importance of faith into my belief system, and I have picked up that baton to pass on the teachings and promises of the Word of God to my family and community.

My father and mother had tremendous work ethics before they retired, allowing them to achieve middle class as young adults. Both grew up in rural towns on working farms, setting the foundation of how they viewed labor. My parents had full-time jobs during my formative years—my father in a steel mill and my mother at an oil company. They were devoted church leaders who believed the whole family should go to church almost every day: Sunday school, Sunday morning service, Sunday evening service, Wednesday night prayer meetings, Vacation Bible School ... you get the picture.

However, with all the good intentions and parental examples, our blended family was not the ideal melting pot. My dad was married before he met my mom and conceived four beautiful children: my step-sister and three step-brothers. The merging of the three older kids with my little brother and myself was not as easy or peaceful as my parents had hoped. There was always some sort of disturbance at our home. Perceptions of unfairness, unequal love, and uneven wealth distribution kept us fractured. Unfortunately, these cracks continue to deepen today. My people have experienced the traumas of drugs, alcohol, and sexual addiction. We have survived prison, suicide, and physical abuse. We could write a Lifetime movie! I will not expose much of my family drama as it's unfair to other family members. But now you can see why I'm driven to leave a certain type of legacy for my immediate family and be an example to households worldwide. Family legacies are so powerful they can affect you in a good or bad way for your whole life. I am determined not to allow my past to dictate my present or my future.

Today, I am married for the second and final time with my own blended family. My husband had three lovely daughters before we met. While my first marriage did not yield any offspring, the privilege of helping to raise my bonus daughters has provided all the motherly "feels" I desire. I love them dearly as if they were my own, and they look to me as a mother figure. My life is an example to them. While the girls have strong relationships with their biological father and mother, I realize my job is just as important as an extension of the family leadership team. I have happily invested my time, resources, and money into the girls' lives to ensure they understand family is love, no matter how the bond was formed.

This is a lesson I learned growing up in a merged household. It is a principle passed down to me from my mother. I sculpted it in my own way and passed it down to my stepdaughters. Strong family roots are not just tied to blood; they grow where the seeds are planted, tilled, and fertilized. Healthy family trees are so important to a successful life—the responsibilities cannot be taken lightly. Autopilot has no place here. Our responsibility is to lean into our habits and behaviors and adjust them if they are unproductive.

Your family is the perfect place to begin your strong legacy, as it sets the foundation for giving. As children, we learn the basic principles of giving by sharing our toys, candy, playtime, and other coveted items with close relatives and little friends. As adults, we develop an advanced concept of giving by making more independent decisions on what to share and with whom. Legacy is an advanced concept of giving as we intentionally leave an inheritance that impacts another person's life. An inheritance can be a gift that enriches someone's life, like heart-healthy recipes left by a loving grandmother. It can also be a burden that weighs someone down, like an embarrassing reputation that has tarnished the family name.

My ascendants left an overall favorable inheritance for me. Now, it's my duty to build on their foundation and layer a step higher for those who come after me. It's an expectation from God. "*A good person leaves an inheritance for their children's children …* " (Prov. 13:22 NIV). The legacy I leave is tied to my existence. I have experienced decent success in my professional life, found love again, and hit many travel locations on my bucket list. In the midst of my journey, I have been committed to passing on an uplifting intergenerational impact. To boost my efforts, I have studied, written, planned, surveyed, and practiced legacy living. As a legacy liver, I keep my end goals in mind as I stretch towards my desires and dreams—how I want to be remembered, what I give back to the community, and what I will leave my family.

As a certified life coach specializing in legacy development, I am on a mission to elevate and advance families using my passion to enhance my own family through legacy living. I feel a sense of responsibility to share strategies to uplift other families as I discover ways to elevate my own.

Some people will caution that focusing on your legacy is selfish, and those who leave one are vain to want to be remembered forever. I argue that it is selfish not to concern yourself with helping others. Your legacy could be that powerful thing that breaks a family cycle. It could be the one thing that saves a child from a lifetime of pain. Consider the gift that you leave the world a beautifully wrapped box with a bow. Your name is just a tag on the gift used for reference. Anything you pass to the future should be an unselfish offering focusing on leaving this world better than it was. Do not let anyone stop you from playing your vital part. We all need your gifts, talents, and offerings. We all need your legacy.

Chapter 2:
Powerful

Always remember this: you are powerful! Stop and let that soak in. You have the power and authority to change circumstances. We were created to have dominion over all earthly things. Genesis 1: 27–28 (NIV) says:

> So God created mankind in his own image, in the image of God he created them; male and female he created them. God blessed them and said to them, "Be fruitful and increase in number; fill the earth and subdue it. Rule over the fish in the seas and the birds in the sky and over every living creature that moves on the ground."

We are the head honcho of the species line. God gave us the cognitive ability to control it all. Our heavenly Father equipped us with high-capacity brains to form complex thoughts, reasoning skills, expansive language, and the power to make things happen. So, give yourself unlimited permission to unleash your power, for goodness' sake.

The grey matter comfortably lounging in your head has billions of nerve cells forming a pattern to coordinate your thoughts, emotions, and behavior. As you read these words, electrical impulses carry messages through your nerve cells at lightning speed so you can comprehend what you see on this page.[1] At the same time, your brain orchestrates your eye movements, your mouth curve, your hand sequences, what you hear, your breathing, and so much more. Imagining all of this happening at once is mind-blowing yet inspiring. Just envisioning what a mind can do feels empowering.

Our thoughts are so strong they form the fundamental principles of our beliefs. They determine our core values and our faith. Our minds form an unstoppable synergistic force when partnered with action. It can lift you to new heights physically, mentally, and emotionally. According to the Laboratory of Neuro Imaging at the University of Southern California, the average brain generates 48.6 thoughts per minute. This adds up to a total of 70,000 thoughts per day. If you discipline your mind to focus just a third of those thoughts on positive things and action plans to reach your goals, imagine how productive you will be.

By that same concept, your mind can drag you down and take you to deep lows. Allowing negativity to seep into your head can wreak havoc on your life, stealing your confidence and crushing your spirit. Unfortunately, of the thousands of thoughts a person has every day, it's estimated that 70 percent of this mental chatter is negative.[2]

Negative self-talk can sneak into our daily habits in many ways, from obsessing over bad past experiences to constantly gazing at social media. It's important to consistently guard ourselves against negative activities we cannot control, and instead, we should discipline our consciousness to focus on things that are within our power. Of course, it's unrealistic to think we can avoid our past or social media altogether, but we can limit our intake.

For instance, if you notice you can't stop asking why things happened in your past, start training your mind to shift to how you may prevent others from going through the same traumas. Or, if you feel

---

2   Alban, Patrick. "72 Amazing Human Brain Facts (Based on the Latest Science)." Be Brain Fit, September 21, 2022. https://bebrainfit.com/human-brain-facts/.

social media is encouraging you to focus on worldly aspects that are not positively aligned with your mission or purpose, set it aside and affirm your goals. Grab a book or journal to reawaken your life's brighter aspects. If something takes you off track or gets too heavy, train your mind to recognize this trap and redirect your energy to things you can control. Regardless of how ugly you've allowed your deepest thoughts to go, your mind has the capability to transport you to higher places and the muscle to move you forward. This is a great way to tap into your power, a God-given gift, to pursue the intended purpose of your life.

The concept behind manifesting is teaching your mind to pivot from the negative to the positive. Manifesters believe we can have what we want if we allow ourselves to think deeply about our desires to the point of envisioning every single detail. It is believed that your actions will follow wherever you put your mind. How to manifest has steadily risen to the top of Google searches in the last five years, according to a Self.com April 2022 article. The author, Mara Santilli, writes, "This increased popularity makes sense considering our experience of coping with a global pandemic ... during which we've experienced a collective lack of control, and for many of us, plenty of extra time to reflect on what matters most to us."[3]

While many mental health experts say manifesting does not work, some people swear by it, saying it has given them exactly what they hoped for. Whether it works or not, the concept of manifestation confirms our minds' strength and vast capacity. We all understand that powerful things can happen if we fasten our minds to a particular goal.

Legacy living manifests when we intentionally challenge our thought process to make each day count towards vision for our lives

---

3   Santilli, Mara. "Psychology Experts on Whether Manifesting Actually Works." SELF, April 22, 2022. https://www.self.com/story/does-manifesting-work.

and the vision others will have of us when we die. Contrary to what some may believe, it is worthwhile to concentrate on what mark you will leave once you depart this world. It is only narcissistic if we merely think of ourselves and not the needs of others. For example, it's vanity to donate money to have a building named after yourself and not care how the structure will benefit others. However, suppose you donate a building to improve the lives of others and have your family carry on this tradition. In that case, you are working in the spirit of a positive, impactful legacy. Remember, we all leave a mark; whether good or bad, lasting or fleeting, it's up to you.

In all walks of life, an impactful legacy is something to aim for. It is confirmation that you've lived well and set up future heirs to do the same.

For Christians, leaving a good legacy is biblical. Proverbs 13:22 (NIV) says, "*A good person leaves an inheritance for their children's children....* " More than 200 passages in the Old and New Testaments speak of inheritance. The greatest inheritance for believers is eternal life in heaven through the grace of Jesus Christ.

For Buddhists, there are two kinds of inheritance. One, children inherit teachings from their parents to restrain from evil, do good, prepare them for a profession, arrange a suitable marriage, and at the proper time, wealth. The second is the inheritance of Kamma, in which a soul never truly dies—it's in a perpetual cycle of birth and death. It lives on through different souls.

For Muslims, the laws of inheritance come from Allah himself, according to the Qur'an. Both men and women can inherit property from their parents, but there are guiding principles according to the family's bloodline.

As you can see, inheritance is monumental in most faith-based belief systems. In the world's top three most practiced religions, it is crucial to the cultural and spiritual survival of the next generation.

Some think if you don't have a well-recognized, broad-range legacy, your contributions are minuscule and won't matter. This is not true, of course. Smaller contributions make a world of difference. Every little favorable act has the potential to build into a more significant, positive force that continues to grow as more people contribute good deeds.

It's one of the greatest examples of the butterfly effect. One soft flap of a butterfly wing can snowball into a cosmic event, resulting in idealistic change reaching the ends of the earth. Just imagine what your small gesture could do. Imagine if we all flapped our wings in a positive direction—how that could change a child's trajectory, a single mother's plight, a man's future, and a family's wealth.

I have a purpose statement on my laundry room/office desk. It reminds me to "elevate and advance families of color." If there is a way to achieve this mission, even in a small way, that is where I should go. I have fastened my mind to it.

While my stepdaughters did not come to this world through my birth canal, they are an intricate part of me. I am committed to ensuring they are well-equipped to live productive lives. My girls are my family through marriage but are part of my legacy by choice. I will fight to protect them and allow them to climb on my shoulders to lift them to heights I myself have never experienced. I want them to soar towards their dreams so they can also serve as an example to their children and their children's children. I have committed my time, thoughts, and finances to the cause.

I have several family and friends who admirably uplift communities through their foundations, raising funds for those less fortunate and hoping for a better life. They strongly believe they have a duty to enhance humankind. I thank God for them and their commitment to elevate others. I feel honored to be around them and their legacy-driven mindsets as they remind me of the important things in life. They are powerful. And they have uncovered the superpower that fuels their mission.

My husband, Micheal "Mike" Williams, has also tapped the power of his mind. He played professional basketball for 11 years and is a great example of a man mentally committed to leaving a lasting legacy. Playing a professional sport for more than a decade is no small feat. Keeping your head in the game and your body in tip-top shape takes a mental toughness that few understand. But even more impressive, when Mike retired from the NBA, he left the game, but he brought with him a drive and competitiveness that would lead him to open his own construction company. Mike could have kicked up his heels and played golf every day for the rest of his life. Instead, he formed 3i Contracting, a Dallas, Texas-based general contracting firm that builds schools, churches, and other public and private structures. As Mike developed strong relationships with Dallas communities through his company, he noticed an unmet need that could advance future construction workers from low-income neighborhoods before they even entered the workforce. Mike formed a non-profit foundation called Mike Williams Assist 4 Life, which prepares high schoolers to enter the construction industry as leaders. The skills taught within the Assist 4 Life program position students for better pay when they enter the industry, a vital lifeline needed for the financial stability of future families. Assist 4 Life is working with one of the largest school districts in Texas with plans to expand. The program has touched students ranging from ninth through twelfth grades—just a drop in the bucket, but a magnificent start.

Remember how incredibly powerful you are as you think through your legacy goals. That voice in your head, that desire in your heart, that vision you keep seeing whenever you daydream—it's quite possibly a divine sign to get moving in the right direction. The path of your dutiful legacy awaits.

Combine your mental capacity with your desire to extinguish unhealthy familial patterns and surge toward new hope and heights. There is so much proof that a disciplined mind can have an incredible impact. In the next chapter, you will read about two types of legacies and discover regular people like you and me who have disrupted the norm to leave a legacy that matters.

Part 2
Exemplify

If you can't figure out your purpose, figure out your passion.
For your passion will lead you right to your purpose.

—T.D. Jakes, *missionary and faith-based leader*

Chapter 3:
Types of Legacies

You don't have to be a genius with Einstein's IQ to leave a lasting legacy. It doesn't require swollen pockets filled with money to pass on a financial inheritance to your family, community, or the world. You just need to be rich with actions, deeds, and a desire to make a difference. There are many different ways to leave a lasting generational impression. Take some time to think through the needs of those around you, coupled with what would make you proud, and violà, you have a winning combination. We discuss clearly defining your legacy in Chapter 14—in the meantime, let's look at the two types of legacies: Footprints and "Heartprints."

Footprint

Most people envision money, land, or other tangible things when they think of legacies or inheritances. These gifts are considered a footprint legacy. Footprint legacies are comprised of those things we can see or touch. Footprints include physical items like houses and other buildings, cars, money, jewelry, etc. Footprint gifts are meant to increase your heirs' wealth and build monetary stability, providing economic relief or financial independence. Footprint gifts can also catalyze community improvement, using donated land to build parks, or grants to provide playground equipment, ponds, and seating, for instance. Leaving a footprint is crucial to generational wealth and community survival.

Heartprint

While a footprint is an essential type of inheritance, you can leave other less tangible items to your family and community just as important as money. A "heartprint" gift can be a powerful asset regarding family and community character and principles. Heartprints are presents you can feel and believe. Heartprints encompass non-tangible items like spiritual faith, values, good work ethic, written stories, poems, family recipes, family history, heirlooms, etc. Popular examples of heartprint legacies include the American flag by Betsy Ross. While the stars and stripes design is tangible, the social currency comes from the rich beliefs and principles the flag represents.

Another example is the Bible, the best-selling book of all time. According to Alltopeverything.com, more than 5 billion copies of the Bible have been sold as of 2022. Not only will the names of the authors and characters in the Bible live on forever, but their experiences and testimonies guide how Christians live and what we believe. The heartprint left by Dr. Martin Luther King Jr., who gave his life to fight for inequality peacefully, is one of American's favorite inheritances. Dr. King's marches and speeches have carved their way into American history, and his life's purpose of abolishing Jim Crow laws affected a nation of millions until the end of time.

Those are extremely popular illustrations, but there are many lesser-known heartprint legacies passed down through generations. For instance, Carolyn Quick Tillery's *The African American Heritage Cookbook*, published in 1997, has become my favorite instructional soul food "go-to." Tillery gathered a collection of southern recipes reminiscent of the smells of Tuskegee Institute in Alabama during Booker T. Washington's reign. Interwoven within recipes like "My Grandmother's Pound Cake" are memories and literary passages describing the pride and suffering of students, educators, and families whose lives were touched by the school for Blacks. The perfect combination of smells, tastes, and history brings the down-home recipes to life. I plan to pass this recipe book (with my handwritten additions) to one of my family members who loves cooking. I hope to keep it in the family.

Some of the best legacies include both footprints and heartprints. The Bill & Melinda Gates Foundation has given away more than $36 billion as of 2022. The foundation says the funds have helped cure diseases, saved lives, and fought poverty. According to the Living to Give Organization, television tycoon Oprah Winfrey has raised over $80 million to establish 60 schools in 13 countries. She has given more to colleges and public schools to help uplift, inspire, and empower women and children. There are many other high-profile examples.

While famous, uber-wealthy, and super smart people gain attention for their contributions, there are less famous people with little wealth who have left an enormous impact, just as critical to our communities. In the following five chapters, I highlight people like you and me who have disrupted the normal flow of everyday life and created a path to leave significant legacies. These stories are important because they show that everyone has a part to play. We're all contributing to a higher cause, larger than us. Mother Theresa, the most famous nun of recent times, said it best: "I alone cannot change the world, but I can cast a stone across the waters to create many ripples." Ripples can form a wave. Combined with other waves, before we know it, we're surfing high above an ocean.

Chapter 4:
A Legacy Leaver: Oseola McCarty of Mississippi

I will never forget the story of Oseola McCarty of Hattiesburg, Mississippi. McCarty was raised by her aunt and grandmother, who cooked, cleaned house, and washed clothes to take care of her. They earned wages for a meager living in the early 1900s. In the sixth grade, it was McCarty's turn to help care for the household. Although she dreamed of becoming a nurse, McCarty had to drop out of school to help take care of her sick aunt. McCarty earned a living the same way her aunt and grandmother did: providing domestic work as a washer and seamstress. For years, she deposited a portion of her small wages into a savings account without touching the funds, not even for an air conditioner during the sweltering summers in the south. McCarty never married or had children. She lived her adult life alone in a small wooden framed house and never owned or drove a car. Her world consisted of the grocery store and church, all within walking distance from her home.

At age 88, three years before she passed away, McCarty decided to give away much of her life savings. She amassed more than $250,000 in savings over the 70 years she worked, $150,000 of which she endowed to the University of Southern Mississippi for African-American students who would otherwise not have funds to attend the college. McCarty spoke of her fortune to *The New York Times* in 1995: "I'm giving it away so that the children won't have to work so hard, like I did." McCarty's donation of $150,000 to the University of Southern Mississippi is the largest gift given by an African-American to this university. McCarty's incredible donation inspired others to contribute scholarships to African-American students at USM. The fund McCarty started raised an additional $330,000 through 600 other donors.

This clothes washer from Mississippi gained worldwide attention as the symbol of selfless giving. McCarty met President Bill Clinton and was honored by the United Nations. She received the Presidential Citizen's Medal, the nation's second-highest civilian award, and honorary degrees from USM and Harvard University. McCarty's legacy lives on through the Oseola McCarty Scholars Program and the many students she helped to complete college, even though she never made it past elementary school.

Chapter 5:
A Legacy Leaving Child: Alex's Lemonade Stand

A remarkable legacy of a child, Alexandra "Alex" Scott was born on January 18, 1996, the second of four children. Shortly before her first birthday, Alex was diagnosed with neuroblastoma, a type of childhood cancer. In 2000, the day after her fourth birthday, Alex received a stem cell transplant. She told her mother, Liz Scott, "When I get out of the hospital, I want to have a lemonade stand." Alex wanted to give the money to doctors to allow them to "help other kids like they helped me." True to her word, she opened her first lemonade stand later that year with the help of her older brother and raised an amazing $2,000 for "her hospital."

While bravely battling her own cancer, Alex and her family continued to hold yearly lemonade stands in their front yard to benefit childhood cancer research. News spread of the generous work little Alex was doing to help other sick children. People inspired by one little girl's mission created their own lemonade stands and donated the proceeds to Alex and her cause.

Alex passed away in August 2004 at the age of eight. Before she died, she realized her persistent work had paid off as she raised more than $1 million to help find a cure for the disease that took her life. Alex's family and supporters around the world are committed to continuing her inspiring legacy through Alex's Lemonade Stand Foundation. You can learn more at alexslemonade.org.

Chapter 6:
A Legacy Leaver: Football to Farm

During his heyday, he was the highest-paid center in the National Football League. But former NFL center lineman Jason Brown gave up a lucrative multi-million dollar career to pursue a higher calling at age 29. His dream was to feed the hungry. Brown moved his wife and eight children out of their 10,000-square-foot St. Louis mansion and swapped it for a farmhouse in North Carolina near land his grandfather farmed decades before, according to *Black Enterprise* (March 3, 2022).

Brown and his wife, Tay, established First Fruits Farm in Franklin County, North Carolina, in April 2012. A 1,000–acre property incorporated under the family's Christian ministry, Wisdom for Life, to share the gospel of Jesus Christ. To cultivate the land, Brown learned the basics of farming on YouTube, and harvesting opportunities were made possible through partnerships with the Society of St. Andrews, the Interfaith Food Shuttle, and the Food Bank of Eastern North. These collaborative efforts saw more than 10,000 pounds of cucumbers and 100,000 pounds of sweet potatoes, all donated to local hunger relief efforts.

First Fruits Farm has contributed over a million pounds of food. "Seeing my children when we are out there in the farm field and knowing that they're learning life skills to help feed them and their families for generations to come, that is the blessing of a farm," Brown said in an interview with the *TODAY* show. He added, "Before, I had to wrestle 300–pound defensive linemen. Now I have to wrestle 1,000–pound cows!"[4]

---

[4] "'In God There Is No Failure': The Leap of Faith a Millionaire NFL Star Took That Landed Him on a Farm in NC." ABC11 Raleigh-Durham, February 11, 2021. https://abc11.com/jason-brown-farming-nfl-business/10326205/.

Chapter 7:
A Legacy Leaver: Lucy Ann Jackson

Enslaved the first 40–plus years of her life, Lucy Ann Jackson was named the "oldest American voter" by the Columbia Broadcasting System on an election night, Tuesday, November 3, 1936. At the ripe age of 114, Jackson walked to the post office in Tarrytown, New York, in her words, "under my own steam" to register to vote for the president of the United States. She was born and raised on plantations in Nelson County, Virginia, until the end of the Civil War. Jackson, who lived with one of her children, rose to fame in her small town where she voted. A newspaper reporter assigned to gather details for an article noted:

> *The assignment to interview a woman more than a century old conjures visions in the mind of a frail figure reclining in bed looking back through the corridors of time with little inclination or ability to talk about life and its milestones.... But, walking in the door of Mr. Carrie Richardson's home ... no bed or invalid chair was pointed out. There was Mrs. Jackson, at the age of 114, busily mending a pair of trousers with quick accurate strokes of the needle.*[5]

---

5   Phillip, Nicole. "Stories from Slavery, Shared Over Generations." *The New York Times*, October 29, 2019. https://www.nytimes.com/interactive/2019/10/29/magazine/family-history-slavery.html.

Jackson told another newspaper reporter she had never had a serious illness in her life and had never seen a doctor. She added, "Don't worry, work hard and take care of your health."[6]

---

[6] "Celebrating Local Black History." The Historical Society, Inc. Accessed February 3, 2024. https://www.thehistoricalsociety.net/history/celebrating-local-black-history/.

Chapter 8:
A Legacy Leaver: Avi Schiffman

At 17 years old, Avi Schiffman, a Washington state high school student, heard about the coronavirus in China. Even before any cases were reported in the United States, Schiffman created a website to track the spread of COVID-19, not just in China but across the world. What remarkable foresight. Tens of millions of people from around the world have visited his site. In fact, ncov2019.live is still tracking the virus today. Schiffman says he has about 30 million visitors a day.

There's something unique about Schiffman's database. It tracks the number of people who have recovered from COVID-19 as well as serious cases and related deaths.[7] Schiffman taught himself how to code using YouTube videos at the tender age of seven. After Schiffman's website became a viral sensation, he was offered $8 million to place ads on the site, but the youngster turned it down. Now, he's working on a new website focused on the conflict in Ukraine. His goal is to help affected refugees find a safe place to stay in neighboring countries and other places around the world.[8]

---

7   O'Brien, essen. "Inspiring Teens Who Changed the World Before 20." JanSport, March 22, 2021. https://www.jansport.com/blogs/inspiring-teens-who-changed-the-world.html.
8   Schlosser, Kurt. "Viral Sensation: Seattle Kid Who Built Coronavirus

Website Catches Eye of a Top Twitter Tastemaker." GeekWire, April 8, 2020. https://www.geekwire.com/2020/viral-sensation-seattle-kid-built-coronavirus-website-catches-eye-top-twitter-tastemaker/.

Chapter 9:
Weird Legacies & Inheritances

I couldn't end this section without acknowledging some of the most interesting and strangest gifts left behind. As I researched inspiring legacies, I stumbled upon uniquely thoughtful, weird, and kooky handouts. You won't believe some of these well-planned and funded inheritances. Either these grantors have a strange sense of humor, or they just plan well. I won't judge here. Read for yourself.

The Incredible Inheritance of Gunther III

In 1992, Gunther III inherited a whopping $80 million from Countess Karlotta Leibenstein. The will included a nine-bedroom, eight-and-a-half-bathroom waterfront estate in Miami, Florida, once occupied by Madonna. The Countess had no children or close relatives, so she left her fortune to her best friend, her beloved German shepherd. That's right, Gunther III is a dog. The pooch slept in the sprawling master bedroom after the Countess passed and had the run of the house. Gunther III's wealth has been passed down to his descendants. Now, Gunther III's grandson, Gunther VI, is enjoying the pampered life. His estate is worth an estimated $500 million today.[9]

9	Marx, Linda. "World's Wealthiest Dog (Yes, Dog!) Sells Madonna's Former Miami Mansion for $29 Million." Peoplemag, January 3, 2022. https://people.com/home/the-worlds-wealthiest-dog-gunther-vi-lists-his-miami-vacation-home-

An Insulting Inheritance

English nobleman and politician Philip Herbert, fifth Earl of Pembroke and second Earl of Montgomery, was a high society noble through his family's bloodline in the mid-1600s. His father, the fourth Earl of Pembroke, was favored by King James I and was given many gifts, including prominent titles and positions like Knight of Garter. While the fifth Earl of Pembroke was less distinguished than his father, he did leave a lasting impression with his Last Will and Testament to one of his nemeses. "I give to Lieutenant-General Cromwell one of my words ... which he must want, seeing as he hath never kept one of his own."[10] Who knew there was so much shade back in the 17th century?

Freakish Legacy

The inventor of the Frisbee, Ed Headrick, wanted to be cremated when he died. He invented the Frisbee in the 1950s, then created the sport disc golf in the 1970s. Headrick was so into the Frisbee that, according to his family, his final wish was to turn his ashes into a Frisbee. His son said it was his father's dream that they play with him after death and even jokingly added that he might even accidentally end up on someone's roof.[11]

---

that-once-belonged-to-madonna-for-31-75-million/.

10   *The New York Times Magazine*, "About Mean: Last Will and Testament," by Williams D. Zabel, May 20, 1984, Section 6, Page 82. nytimes.com/1984/05/20/magazine.

11   Tayor, Daniel. "Morning Start: The Inventor of the Frisbee Turned Into a Frisbee After He Died." Vernon Morning Star, 2020. https://www.vernonmorningstar.com/news/morning-start-the-inventor-of-the-frisbee-turned-into-a-frisbee-after-he-died-3312852.

The Eenie, Meenie, Miney, Moe Legacy

Imagine getting a surprise inheritance from someone you don't know. That is what happened to 70 people in Portugal in 2007. According to *The Guardian*, Luis Carlos de Noronha Cabral de Camara was an unhappy, illegitimate son to an aristocratic woman who did not care for him. A nanny raised him. Luis Carlos never married, had few friends, and no children of his own. He passed away young, drunk, and alone. But, 20 years before his death, he asked a Portuguese notary for a copy of the Lisbon phonebook and began arbitrarily picking out names. He randomly chose heirs to receive his valuables. Once he died at 42, people around Lisbon started receiving letters from Luis Carlos's lawyer, letting them know they could now claim a share of his fortune. The unusual benefactor left a 12-room apartment, a house near Guimaraes, a luxury car, two motorbikes, and roughly $32,000. "I thought it was some kind of cruel joke," a 70-year-old heir told a local newspaper. "I'd never heard of the man."[12]

Long-Lasting Loving Legacy

Comedian Jack Benny must have been head over heels in love with his wife, Mary. He arranged to leave daily reminders of his adoration for her before he passed away. Benny was known for his excellent comedic timing and hilarious long pregnant pauses, but after his death in 1974, he became known for a more affectionate matter—leaving behind one of the sweetest gestures of all time. Benny arranged in his Will for his wife to receive one single long-stemmed red rose every day for the rest of her life. Mary received over 3,200 red roses from her late husband before she passed away. I wonder if that inheritance had a dual pur-

---

12   Tremlett, Giles. "Wealthy Loner Picks Heirs From Phone Book." The Guardian, January 16, 2007. https://www.theguardian.com/world/2007/jan/16/gilestremlett.mainsection.

pose because whoever tried to win Mary's heart after Benny passed would have had some stiff competition (literally).[13]

---

[13] Ketchum, Dan. "The Top 15 Strangest Inheritances." GOBankingRates, March 11, 2019. https://www.gobankingrates.com/money/wealth/strangest-inheritances.

Part 3
Give

Legacy is not what I did for myself. It's what I'm doing for the next generation.

—Vitor Belfort, *Brazilian athlete*

Chapter 10:
The Benefits of Giving

In all definitions of legacy, the act of giving is present. Webster's Unabridged Dictionary describes *legacy* as "a gift of property by will, esp. of money or personal property; a bequest." When you receive a legacy, you inherit whatever tangible, intellectual, or intangible properties are left to you. You are an heir. Whenever you contribute something that impacts your descendants, you are a benefactor. You are giving something that should benefit the receiver.

From the beginning of time, our very existence was based on inheritance. In the first book of the Bible, Genesis 1:26 (NIV) says, *"Then God said, 'Let us make mankind in our image, in our likeness, so that they may rule over the fish in the sea and the birds in the sky, over the livestock and all the wild animals, and over all the creatures that move along the ground.'"* God gave us authority over all living things. We are the heirs of all His wondrous creations left for us here on earth.

In fact, we are recipients of the biggest and best inheritance ever known to humankind. God sacrificed His Son's life in a brutal way to show us how much our lives mean to Him. He allowed Jesus to be tortured and beaten, so the overflowing presence of blood would be an unforgettable reminder of our inheritance of everlasting life. *"For God so loved the world that he gave his one and only Son, that whoever believes in him shall not perish but have eternal life"* (John 3:16 NIV).

Inheritance is and always will be an integral part of living and surviving. Those who understand this could have a prosperous family lineage that thrives generation after generation. Psalm 112:1–3 (NIV) says, *"Praise the Lord. Blessed is the man who fears the Lord, who finds great delight in his commands. His children will be mighty in the land; the generation of the upright will be blessed. Wealth and riches are in this house, and his righteousness endures forever."*

Those who fail to provide a good inheritance and indulge in a selfish existence could create a family cycle of struggle and hardships. A good inheritance is such an honorable and valuable gift that when King David prayed against his enemies, he asked God to strip his adversary of any chance of a respectable lineage by cursing his offspring.

Psalm 109:9–15 (NIV):

> *May his children be fatherless*
>   *and his wife a widow.*
> *May his children be wandering beggars;*
>   *may they be driven from their ruined homes.*
> *May a creditor seize all he has;*
>   *may strangers plunder the fruits of his labor.*
> *May no one extend kindness to him*
>   *or take pity on his fatherless children.*
> *May his descendants be cut off,*
>   *their names blotted out from the next generation.*
> *May the iniquity of his fathers be remembered before the Lord;*
>   *may the sin of his mother never be blotted out.*
> *May their sins always remain before the Lord,*
>   *that he may blot out their name from the earth.*

David knew how to hit a man where it hurt. Legacies are a vital equation to generational wealth and stability. It provides a solid foundation for the next generation and enhances a family's quality of life. Whether leaving a footprint or a heartprint, transferring something of value and significance to your heirs is essential. Benefactors must be intentional about what they plan to pass on to their loved ones. Those who are not intentional could perpetuate a bleak future for the next generation.

Unfortunately, there are plenty of examples of unfavorable legacies left behind—some left on purpose, and others from an indifferent mindset. For this book's purpose, we will not focus on negative legacies that were purposeful. You can research and read about spree shooters, serial killers, and other dark individuals who orchestrated infamous tragedies soiling our history. They wanted to be remembered for their evil. If a person is driven to leave a stain on the world, there is little you can do to change that. As I said before, our minds are powerful—whatever you determine to do, you will find a way.

What is sad, however, are those who did not intend to leave adverse legacies but did so by failing to acknowledge the importance of self-examination and planning. Harmful legacies may be created when we don't take the time to evaluate our lives, daily habits, or set goals for ourselves and our families. Damaging legacies of abuse, poverty, criminalization, complacency, hate, racism, or sexism are sometimes handed down through parent-child relationships. For example, a father who was neglected or not shown much affection as a child could pass those feelings of isolation or disconnection to his son by displaying those same behaviors. Or, a mother who was emotionally and physically punished as a child may suffer from low self-esteem or aggression and pass that on to her daughter using those same disciplinary techniques.

These family cycles create negative consequences beyond the immediate family. It affects how we relate to friends and coworkers and has a rippling effect on the community. It is worth the time to sort through unhealthy habits passed on to you to ensure you don't pass them on to others. Seek the help of a therapist or a counselor or make a conscious effort to terminate unhealthy behaviors. The benefit could be two-fold: you could create a healthier you and develop a stronger lineage.

There are many other benefits to leaving a good inheritance. Giving communicates that you care about your loved ones and their well-being, which builds trust, strengthens family relationships, and provides a sense of security. Giving can also have a positive impact on society. When we give to charitable organizations or support causes we believe in, we are addressing important social issues that make a difference in the world.

Giving not only helps our family and society, but it's also scientifically proven that it benefits your well-being. Studies have shown that people who give to others experience greater happiness and satisfaction.[14] This backs the familiar saying, "It is better to give than receive."[15] Generosity reduces stress and improves your overall health. Dr. Susan Albers-Bowling, a psychologist with the Cleveland Clinic, says donating can boost your physical and mental health—a chemical response occurs in your body when you do something nice. Research shows that during the act of giving, you release serotonin, which regulates your mood; dopamine, which gives you a sense of pleasure; and oxytocin, which creates a sense of connection with others. When your brain secretes these hormones, it can lower your blood pressure by inhibiting the release of norepinephrine, which decreases your heart rate.

---

14 Albers, Susan. "Why Giving Is Good for Your Health." Cleveland Clinic, January 5, 2023. https://health.clevelandclinic.org/why-giving-is-good-for-your-health.

15 "What Are the Health Benefits of Altruism?" Mental Health Foundation. Accessed October 5, 2023. https://www.mentalhealth.org.uk/explore-mental-health/articles/what-are-health-benefits-altruism.

Additionally, people who volunteer tend to live longer than those who do not, says Dr. Albers-Bowling.[16]

Gift giving also melts away stress because it reduces cortisol levels, the molecules that make you feel overwhelmed and anxious. It also stimulates your brain's reward center by releasing endorphins that boost self-esteem and combats depression.[17]

Another benefit is that helping others distracts us from our own problems. "Many people don't realize the impact that a different perspective can have on their outlook on life," reports an article called "The Benefits of Serving Others."[18] "Helping others in need can provide a real sense of perspective and make you realize how lucky you are." We all know someone who has hyper-focused on a negative occurrence that happened to them. They can't get their mind off the issue. They constantly talk about it, and every conversation leads to the same thing: the negative issue. Maybe this was you at some point in time.

I remember having a fit when I was 16 because my father got me the ugliest, oldest, gas-guzzling hooptie that would shut down at a traffic light just as the light turned green. When I wasn't out driving the clinker, I tried to make my parents feel miserable about giving me the junk on wheels by constantly pouting. My friends even got fed up with my complaints and volunteered to drive everywhere just to shut me up. One day, my mom said, "You need to go volunteer. Go help people who are less fortunate than you." I thought, *What does that have to do with you getting me a better car?* I didn't get it then, but I definitely understand now. Some 16–year-olds (or even adults) would

---

16 Albers, Susan. "Why Giving Is Good for Your Health." Cleveland Clinic, January 5, 2023. https://health.clevelandclinic.org/why-giving-is-good-for-your-health.
17 Ibid.
18 "The Benefits of Serving Others." Quality Healthcare, December 5, 2022. https://www.qualityhealthcare.com.au/post/2019/07/24/the-benefits-of-serving-others.

have been ecstatic to have my jalopy, especially given to them for free. I would have gained that perspective had I followed my mother's orders. Helping someone in need would have distracted me from my silly tantrums, given me a different outlook on my circumstances, and probably given me reasons to be grateful. In my adult years, I understand the importance of reframing my circumstances. Taking a mental break from my issues allows me to approach my situation with fresh and often grateful eyes.

While there are many rewards in giving to others, be cautious if your primary purpose for giving is solely that, as it may lead to severe disappointment. Benevolent giving should have no strings attached, which means that you should not give to get back. There are times when giving could feel lonely or thankless. It can appear one-sided, and the benefactor may perceive they are being exploited or unappreciated. According to *Psychology Today*, in these cases, the giver is often not looking for a return gift in kind but rather some form of recognition or appreciation. The absence of such attention can leave deep wounds to the hopeful giver.[19] It could prevent the benefactor from giving in the future. Instead of getting discouraged, remember that giving should be a selfless act. Find your energy in reminding yourself of the importance of what you are doing and how many lives you could touch.

Better yet, staying tied to faith-based reasons for giving will keep us grounded, releasing ourselves from human expectations and focusing on giving glory to the Almighty. Biblically, our catalyst for giving should be linked to one of the following:

- Love for God
- Gratitude

---

19   Rosenblatt, Therese. "Is Gift Giving a Bad Idea?" *Psychology Today*, 2021. https://www.psychologytoday.com/us/blog/inside-real-peoples-heads/202112/is-gift-giving-bad-idea.

- Recognition that everything we have comes from God
- Desire to be obedient
- Belief in His promises regarding generosity[20]

If we feel underappreciated or justify why we should not give or believe someone does not deserve our goodwill, we should reconcile our thoughts with God's Word to determine a true direction. Powerful legacies are determined by the daily decisions we make. Some resolutions may require stepping out in faith a little more than others.

As stated in the first chapter, I have chosen to focus my mission on family advancement because my family could have used more support when I was younger. I reflect on conflicting childhood memories of my relationship with my father. My dad, a church pastor, generously gave his time to parishioners but rarely had availability to attend any of my school functions or activities. In fact, he wasn't present at my high school or college graduations because he had "church duties." When my father was absent during these milestone moments, I felt unimportant, unseen, and unworthy of his love and energy. As a child, I only saw what he was *not* doing for me versus what he was doing for others. There was little communication about why my father could not make himself available for my important events or ceremonies. It was understood that he had pressing responsibilities more important than supporting his children. My family catered to my father, and everyone else, including my mother, took the sidelines so my dad could focus on ministry. It seemed normal back then, but as I saw other family dynamics, I realized it wasn't. As I analyzed the details of those days, I knew this was a dysfunctional way to raise a family and vowed that whomever I married would commit to family first and everything else

---

20 Calvert, Gina. "8 'Giving' Bible Verses for Growing a Generous Spirit." Vision2, 2023. https://vision2.com/blog/how-to-increase-generosity-at-church.

would be secondary. Charity starts at home. First Timothy 5:8 (NIV) says, *"Anyone who does not provide for their relatives, and especially for their own household, has denied the faith and is worse than an unbeliever."* If you don't focus on raising a healthy family, your work in the community means nothing. Besides, your children are part of the community. If you have not invested in them, you have not helped the community.

In our golden years, where and with whom we should spend our time becomes clear. *Forbes* magazine published a survey in February of 2019 asking men and women 55 and older what they wanted to be remembered for. An astonishing 69 percent of survey respondents said they most want to be remembered for "the memories I've shared with my loved ones." By contrast, only 9 percent said "career success," and 4 percent said "accumulated wealth." Incidentally, these views were pretty consistent among respondents at all income levels. Other responses were "making an impact on society" and "having a great career." This research shows when we get older, most of us want to be known for the precious moments and quality time we've spent with family and close friends.

The personal gratification we gain from giving can be so beneficial that we should all explore various ways to be benevolent. Some of the ways we can give are spiritual in nature.

The next chapter will focus on spiritual gifts and how they align with giving. Sharing our God-given talents with people around us is another way to be charitable and build a legacy worth leaving to the world.

Chapter 11:
Gifts

Spiritual gifts are God-given talents.

These talents are called gifts because we do not work for them. God blesses us with these abilities. While we didn't do anything special to receive our gifts, we do have a significant assignment connected to them. God blesses us with gifts, not to squirrel away for ourselves but to humbly share with others. Unlike a birthday present handed to us for our personal enjoyment, we unwrap spiritual gifts to encourage and uplift people around us. First Peter 4:10 says that each of us should use whatever gift we have received to serve others as faithful stewards of God's grace in its various forms.

Using our spiritual gifts gives us tools to accomplish our life's mission. They help us fulfill our purpose of serving God through caring for each other. Each of us is a small piece of a very large puzzle. First Corinthians 12:14–17 (NIV) says:

> *Even so, the body is not made up of one part but of many. Now, if the foot should say, "Because I am not a hand, I do not belong to the body," it would not for that reason, stop being part of the body. And if the ear should say, "Because I am not an eye, I do not belong to the body," it would not for that reason stop being part of the body. If the whole body were an eye, where would the sense of hearing be? If the whole body were an ear, where would the sense of smell be?*

The Bible often explains the significance of using individual skills to work together. Almost from the very beginning, *"the Lord God said, 'It is not good for the man to be alone. I will make a helper suitable for him'"* (Gen. 2:18 NIV). Throughout the Old and New Testaments, there are mentions of teamwork. Including Ecclesiastes 4:9–12 (NIV):

> *Two are better than one, because they have a good return for their labor: If either of them falls down, one can help the other up. But pity anyone who falls and has no one to help them up. Also, if two lie down together, they will keep warm. But how can one keep warm alone? Though one may be overpowered, two can defend themselves. A cord of three strands is not quickly broken.*

Each of us has different gifts that, when combined, elevate each other to serve a larger purpose. Knowing our gifts helps us understand our purpose. And when we understand our purpose, our legacy becomes clear. Our purpose guides our legacy. Our talents, purpose, and legacies are all intertwined and work hand in hand. Without our abilities, we may not have the aptitude to reach our purpose. Without purpose, we may not leave behind what our heirs need for a successful future. Ephesians 4:16 (NIV) says, *"From him, the whole body, joined and held together by every supporting ligament, grows and builds itself up in love, as each part does its work."* We must identify and understand how to use our gifts in order to fulfill our legacy mission.

Some gifts are easy to identify. Especially artistic skills that require an audience for validation, like someone who has a beautiful voice that mesmerizes a crowd when they sing or speak to our souls or someone who can embody music with body movements bending with the melody of a song through dance, or someone who can take a blank canvas and wow the human eye, conveying language and emotion with colors and lines. But for the rest of us, uncovering our talents may be more of an awakening.

For instance, one of my talents involves communication. I didn't wake up one morning and discover I was good at speaking. It wasn't until I was in the eighth grade that I realized I might be good at vocal expression because one of my teachers told me. Even then, I didn't see it as a talent. I noticed I was not scared to speak in front of people, while some of my other friends shied away from it. It wasn't until I changed my major in college from business to journalism/speech communications that I felt it could be something I could master. I was often told I communicated well before I understood it was a God-given gift.

Through many conversations with others, I realize tons of people have not identified their gifts and constantly wonder what they are good at doing. This is understandable; some talents are less obvious and take discernment to recognize. If you are beginning to uncover your talents, be sure to:

1. Pray that your talents are revealed to you.
2. Ask others, especially family, what you are good at.
3. Identify what you love doing—what brings you joy?
4. Take note of the things you do most.
5. Take some time to meditate on what is revealed to you.

Romans 12:6 talks about seven gifts of the spirit: prophesying, serving, teaching, encouraging, giving, leading, and showing mercy. However, if you search for free self-assessments online to help unveil your spiritual gifts, you will find (on average) 16 to 24 descriptions of spiritual gifts. *Uniquely You* is an organization that helps faith-based groups discover their giftedness. They created a behavioral profile assessment through questions to help uncover your spiritual talents. It lists 16 spiritual gifts collected from Romans 12, Ephesians 4, and 1 Corinthians 12. Here's the list from their website, uniquelyyou.org:

1. Administration / Ruling
2. Apostleship / Pioneering
3. Discernment
4. Encouraging / Exhorting
5. Evangelism
6. Faith
7. Giving
8. Hospitality
9. Knowledge
10. Leadership
11. Pastor / Shepherding
12. Prophecy / Perceiving
13. Teaching
14. Serving / Ministry
15. Showing Mercy
16. Wisdom

There are other free spiritual gift assessments online that list 24 spiritual gifts referencing Romans 12:6–8, 1 Corinthians 12:6–10, 1 Corinthians 12:28, 1 Corinthians 12:29–30, Ephesians 4:11, and 1 Peter 4:11. So, there are several options depending on your preference. I recently took a free spiritual gift assessment online, and my top three gifts were administration, giving, and leadership, which is about right. The site offered a deeper dive for a fee. I declined because I feel comfortable with my gifting; however, for someone just starting to explore their gifts, it may be a good idea. Once you discover your God-given talents, take some time to get to know them. Practice and advance your skills. Then, put them to good use.

Outside the spiritual gifting guides are other books, guides, and online assessments to help provide some perspectives concerning your talents. The Clifton Strength assessment is a popular online questionnaire that helps pinpoint your top strengths. There are 34 categories in the assessment. Once your top five talents are identified, you receive a report describing your abilities and how to use them in your professional and personal life.

The Myers-Briggs Company also offers an assessment that reveals your personal wiring. You can schedule an interview with an MBTI profiler (ideal) or take an online assessment to identify your personality type. Depending on how questions are answered, a participant is placed within one of 16 boxes in a "type table." Each of the 16 boxes describes ways people may behave, their motivations, and their strengths. The type suggested for you (after taking the survey) comes with insights into how you are cognitively wired to interact with your outer and inner worlds. Some of the descriptions include the ability to solve deep problems, being good at reading other people, noticing what people need day to day and trying to provide it for them, being a long-term planner, inspiring leader, and so on. Personal appraisal will enlighten you about things you never paid attention to and help you get closer to acknowledging your skills.

In addition to personal evaluations, consider doing some work on your own. Here are ten suggestions I have summarized from Lifehack.org[21] that encourage us to roll up our sleeves and dig deep within ourselves for exploration:

1. Take time to figure out what makes you feel mentally and emotionally strong. That thing that makes you want to grow

---

21   Romano, Courtney. "13 Ways to Identify Your Talents and Utilize Them." Lifehack, July 18, 2023. https://www.lifehack.org/articles/productivity/10–ways-identify-your-talents-and-utilize-them.html.

yet feel satisfied. Think about what makes you feel happy and gives you a sense of accomplishment when you do it.

2. Look through your finances and see what you spend your money on. Bypass shopping for clothes and shoes for yourself and hone in on other spending patterns over the last year or two. This speaks truth to me because when I look at my finances, I notice trends of buying gifts for others and ensuring my parents receive nice treats. One of my spiritual gifts is gifting, so I'm on target.

3. Gather feedback from your family and friends on your best and not-so-best qualities. They may already have an opinion about your talents, but ask for their thoughts on what you are great at doing. Don't shy away from learning about your worst qualities, too. It will help you narrow your true interests.

4. Get your family to describe what you loved doing as a child. These are people who have known you the longest. Their memories could help you identify long-standing habits or behaviors that are a part of the fabric you may have overlooked. I tried this exercise with my mom, and it was incredibly eye-opening. It appears I've been a communicator all my life. At two years old, I'd walk up to strangers in grocery stores and try to speak a different language to someone (that came out as gibberish). My mom humorously said it was a sign of what was to come.

5. Keep a journal. Observe what you're doing daily and take notes. Also, write about your desires. Go wild with any ideas or thoughts about what you'd like. It's private, so let it rip. Do this consistently whenever a thought comes to mind. After a while, read over your writings. A trend will bubble up. Explore that more until you feel comfortable with a direction.

6. Observe talent in others around you. Use other people in your life for inspiration. Sometimes, watching others work within their gifting triggers inventiveness, leading us to a clearer picture of our natural skills.
7. Consider the items you have collected, like books, music, or movies. Scan your inventory for specific categories you enjoy. Things that ignite excitement, peace, and calm could reveal aspects of your identity because we tend to surround ourselves with what we are attracted to. Dig deeper into this concept to contemplate the allure.
8. What do people thank you most for? Being thanked for something regularly means you are probably good at it. This could be a clue to a talent. It could be anything from being a consistent supporter, strong planner, good listener, or making people laugh; these are all valuable abilities.
9. Keep an open mind for change. Once you believe you've identified your talent, continue to dig within yourself until you have confirmed this. While working within your gift, know that you may have other talents angling to come forward. Don't suppress those desires; stay available to explore those as well. You could very well uncover more than one talent and find one more dominant. This process allows us to stretch and grow, bringing us closer to reaching our full potential.
10. Jump in! Choose the strongest talent you have uncovered and get to work using it. You could find you are extremely satisfied with your gifting, or you may need to return to others on your list to research more. Either way, get started. Don't wait until you are super comfortable with moving forward. You may never feel that way. But, if you don't start, you may never locate your true talents.

Gifts should be used and shared with others, but some folks are not good stewards of their talents or do not use them as God intended. Jesus warned against this during His Sermon on the Mount. Matthew 6:1–2 (NIV) says:

> *Be careful not to practice your righteousness in front of others to be seen by them. If you do, you will have no reward from your Father in heaven. So when you give to the needy, do not announce it with trumpets, as the hypocrites do in the synagogues and on the streets, to be honored by others. Truly I tell you, they have received their reward in full.*

Some people refuse to share their gifts because they are too frightened of failure or rejection. Others use them only for self-gratification and ego adulation. But if your goal is to reach a positive legacy that will increase the lands of your offspring and complete the mission set forth for you here on this earth, you must align with your Higher Power and embrace your role in the overall matrix.

Part 4
Activate

Change makes you find your calling, your legacy, and God's divine plan for your life. Don't run from it.

—Iman, *model and actress*

Chapter 12:
Go

Your desire to construct a legacy that will last through multiple generations can lead to an influence beyond what you ever conceived imaginable. A simple plan could touch many. Even small efforts have the potential to snowball into something epic; that's why it's so important to follow through with those generous ideas. You never know, they could inspire a nation!

This section focuses on several ways to ignite your spirit and propel you to move ahead with those meaningful legacy projects. We'll pull back the curtains to expose a realistic view of where you are in your legacy quest, dive into your life's purpose and mission, see real-world examples of how to leave a favorable legacy, and push you out of your comfort zone and into action.

But first, let's review five fundamental steps[22] to help you get moving with your plans. We will discuss many of these concepts later in the book. However, if you remember nothing else in this section, may these tips sink in and nestle.

1. Start Right Away

It takes time to build a legacy, so make the move now. The sooner you begin, the more time you'll have to intentionally craft your legacy and the longer you'll have to align your actions with your aims. There is

---

22   Mind Tools Content Team. "What Is Legacy Thinking?" MindTools. Accessed October 5, 2023. https://www.mindtools.com/a3axrm1/what-is-legacy-thinking.

rarely a great time to start a new project, so you've got to force yourself to jump in. When you write the pros and cons of what you're working on, legacy impact should top the list. Your impact is that important.

2. Reflect on the Difference You Want to Make

Contemplate the kind of difference you want to make with people. An effective technique (though it may seem slightly morbid) is to draft your own eulogy. Write a speech praising yourself, explaining all the wonderful achievements you've made in your lifetime. Make it a light-hearted, upbeat presentation, and include what you hope your family and friends will say about you after you pass away. If this is too realistic for you, try asking yourself the following questions:

- What values, beliefs, behaviors, strengths, or traits would I like people to remember me for?
- What knowledge or skills would I like to pass on?
- What behaviors do I encourage in other people?
- What do the people around me need? How can I serve them?

Another helpful tip is to consider the inspiration you could draw from others' actions and what you would like to emulate or build on. Research suggests the values or heartprints we leave as a legacy are often more influential than the biological or material legacies we leave.

3. Write a Legacy Statement

Compose a formal legacy statement—a commitment you can refer to often. We will spend an entire chapter on how and why your written declaration of intent is essential. This mission should specify your long-term aspirations and how you want to be remembered.

4. Live Your Legacy

It would be best to start proactively planting seeds for the people around you to leave a good legacy. Now is the time to start aligning your behavior with your mission. Consider what may need to change about your leadership style, behavior, and working methods to ensure your vision is realized.

5. Conduct "Legacy Audits"

This tip is one of my favorites. Even with thoughtful planning, your legacy-building can be fragile; even the slightest crisis or everyday demand could blow it off course. Procrastination or mismanagement could dissolve all the wonderful plans. Be strategic and schedule routine legacy audits to ensure you stay on track. Check in with the people around you; they can help you evaluate your progress. We revisit legacy audits or course corrections towards the end of the book to provide ideas on staying focused and developing resiliency with your plans.

Your actions today can help you clarify what truly matters to you. As you reflect on your values, strengths, and passions, think about how you want to be remembered. Use these insights to build your base, then layer on ways to use your talents to help others. These elements will form your legacy platform, providing a foundation to create a more purposeful life.

Chapter 13:
Legacy Placement Assessment

Understanding the mark you were meant to leave on this earth takes a certain level of self-discovery. If you haven't already, step back and get to know yourself better. Evaluate your spiritual gifts and talents *and* uncover the giving that excites you. Tap into what drives you to understand what pushes you to the edge of your seat. Many of us are stimulated by positive and negative past experiences. For instance, some people feel a calling to feed and clothe those less fortunate because they grew up with food insecurities and without basic necessities. Some feel they were placed here to be a voice for animals because they have witnessed the kindness and loyalty animals give back to humans when treated well. Others may fight for the elderly because they empathize with the fragility of this aging group having observed their grandparents or parents struggle. There are varying stimulants that energize us to take action. What's yours?

Depending on your maturity level, you could still be figuring it out. In the article "The Four Stages of Life," Mark Manson describes periods of consciousness that force us to think about our legacy because we realize we are running out of time.

Stage 1: Mimicry (Birth to early adulthood)
As children, we're wired to learn by watching and mimicking others. We learn physical skills, like how to walk and talk, develop social skills, and adapt to culture.

Stage 2: Self-Discovery (Mid- to late adolescence up to the mid-30s)
In stage one, we learn to fit in with the people and culture around us. Stage two teaches us what makes us different from people and culture. This is the stage where people understand their uniqueness through trial and error. We experiment with people, places, and things to determine what we like and don't like.

Stage 3: Commitment (Mid-30s through retirement)
Once you discover what's important to you, you release undesirable friendships, goals, and habits and double down on healthy relationships, fulfilling work, and reachable goals. Stage three is about maximizing your potential.

Stage 4: Legacy (Mid-50s and beyond)
According to Manson, the focus in stage four is to figure out how to ensure your legacy lasts beyond death. It's when people start thinking about transitioning their finances, business, and wisdom to younger family members and proteges. Manson claims this stage can be challenging to come to grips with because people struggle with their own validity or meaning of life after work and kids.

Manson's stages sound a bit mechanical, with little room for overlap. While I believe we experience different stages in life, there are ways to work towards our legacy through them all. The mechanism lies within uncovering the type of legacy we want to leave. The rest becomes more apparent once we identify what we want to be remembered for.

You don't have to have it all together, lead a perfect existence, or be the wisest person in the room to leave an impact. You just need to commit to a plan and try.

I chose my life mission not because I am super successful at it but because I *want to be*. I strive to be an expert at helping families live out their potential. My mission to advance families of color evolves from personally experiencing and witnessing families with broken spirits due to economic, social, and cultural inequalities and perpetual cycles of dysfunction and selfishness. Whether societal origins or inner turmoil caused the handicaps, destructive intergenerational patterns must be broken for families to thrive. Why not start with me?

Where are you in your quest to leave a positive legacy? Have you thought about it and understand its importance but need help figuring out where to start? I have assembled a legacy assessment using research, experts in the industry, and personal experience that will help pinpoint what you should activate first to get on your legacy path. If you've figured out your purpose, you're halfway there. If you are still looking for the thing that makes you feel fulfilled, I've got a plan for that too.

Be as honest as possible with yourself as you take this evaluation. Its purpose is to give you an idea of where you are versus where you would like to be. Choose the answer that best fits your status right now. You will tally up your score at the end to generate a starting point.

Personal Legacy Placement Assessment

1. How important is it for you to start working on your legacy right now?
   a. Not too important.
   b. It can wait until I'm a little older.
   c. I have started thinking about it.
   d. I am initiating it now.
   e. I have been working on it for a little while.

2. Do you know what type of legacy you want to leave?
   a. No
   b. Yes

3. Have you seriously considered how you want to be remembered once you pass away?
   a. Not really.
   b. I have a general idea.
   c. I am seriously thinking about it now.
   d. I have thought about it and taken action to leave an impact.
   e. I have thought about it, written it down, and am actively working to ensure my vision of who I am resonates with others.

4. Have you told anyone about the type of legacy you want to leave?
   a. No
   b. Yes

5. Have you discussed your legacy with family or close friends?
   a. No
   b. Yes

6. Have you done anything to help define your legacy?
   a. No
   b. Yes

7. Do you have a thorough understanding of inheritance?
   a. No
   b. Yes

8. Do you fully understand how a good inheritance can affect the next generation?
   a. Kind of.
   b. I believe so.
   c. I have done some research on various types of inheritance.
   d. I fully understand how and why a family inheritance can affect the next generation.
   e. I understand how a good inheritance affects family, community, and the world.

9. Do you think it is your duty to leave an inheritance?
   a. Absolutely not.
   b. An inheritance is a gift and can be left if someone chooses.
   c. An inheritance is a duty only if you have something worth leaving.
   d. I think it's my duty to leave an inheritance for my children.
   e. Yes, it's absolutely a must.

10. Do you know who you want to leave an inheritance to?
    a. No.
    b. I have a general idea.
    c. Yes, I know specifically who I want to leave an inheritance to.
    d. I know who I want to leave an inheritance to, and I have told them.
    e. I know who I want to leave an inheritance to, and it is recorded on a written Last Will and Testament.

11. Have you started on a plan to leave a positive legacy?
    a. No.
    b. It can wait until I'm a little older.
    c. I've started thinking about it.
    d. I'm initiating it now.
    e. I've been working on it for a little while.

12. Do you have a written plan to keep you on target for reaching your legacy goals?
    a. No
    b. Yes

13. Is a written plan necessary to leave a positive legacy?
    a. No
    b. Yes

14. Will your legacy plan positively affect the next two to three generations?
    a. I don't know yet.
    b. There is potential for it to affect the next two generations.
    c. I know it will positively affect the next generation, but I don't know about the one after that.
    d. Yes, it should impact the next two generations.
    e. My legacy has been designed to positively impact the next two generations and beyond.

15. Have you identified the legacies you inherited from your ancestors, good or bad, and understand how they have affected your life?
    a. No.
    b. I did not inherit anything from my ancestors.
    c. I am figuring that out now.
    d. I know what I have inherited and have thought through how it has affected my life.
    e. I know my inheritance, understand how it has touched my life, and use those learnings to construct my personal legacy plan.

Turn the page to calculate and review your Legacy Placement Score.

Use the chart on the next page to find your score. Match the question with the letter you chose and write the number. After you have identified the numbers linked with each question, add them together for your score.

Question	A	B	C	D	E
1	10	10	8	5	1
2	10	5			
3	10	8	6	3	1
4	10	5			
5	8	5			
6	10	5			
7	8	5			
8	10	8	6	3	1
9	10	10	6	3	0
10	10	8	5	3	0
11	10	10	6	3	1
12	10	5			
13	10	1			
14	10	8	6	3	0
15	10	10	8	5	1

The higher the score, the more work you need to invest in your plan if your goal is to leave a positive legacy.

If you scored between 36 - 48 points—You are in really good shape. You have thought deeply about what you want to leave the world, and you are legacy living to accomplish your goals.

If you scored between 49 - 59 points—Congratulations, you have taken some key steps to ensure you leave a positive legacy. But don't rest. There is work to be done to strengthen it.

If you scored 60 and above, it's time to consider what you want to achieve, how it will affect future generations, and initiate a plan. If you have a high number, don't feel overwhelmed. Block out some time to continue reading this book. You will find helpful suggestions to get you on your way to legacy living.

You will land in one of three buckets below. Regardless of your status on the chart, the following chapters will provide meaningful considerations for legacy beginners—"Need to get started"; legacy intermediates—"On my way"; and legacy achievers—"Legacy living."

Personal Legacy Placement	Personal Legacy Score
Legacy living	36 - 48 points
On my way	49 - 59 points
Need to get started	60 points and above

Chapter 14:
Self-Discovery

Section 1 – Purpose

Each of us has a purpose; uncovering our assignment opens the door to a more meaningful existence. To unlock our life's mission, we must take a personal journey to reveal deeper knowledge about ourselves. This requires tapping into your uniqueness and embracing your authenticity. Each person's path is different depending on the individual's gifts and talents. Once you enter your purpose-filled realm, you'll operate in your flow where your actions, values, and goals align with your true passions and talents.

If you already know your life's purpose, congratulations! You are a part of the 10 percenters, a very rare club. Research suggests 90 percent of people living today don't know their purpose. And of the ones who do, only 5 percent say they are in touch with their purpose daily.[23] In reality, most people go through their whole lives not knowing their reason for being and never try searching for it. Now, this is a judge-free zone. It's okay if you are satisfied with your life without understanding your purpose. We each have the right to make our own decisions regarding how we live our lives. But if you feel like something is missing or you want to understand how you fit into the greater good, finding your life's mission helps.

---

23   McClung, Aaron. "Finding Purpose: Why It Matters to Your Life and Business." AM Agency, February 16, 2021. https://discoveram.com/finding-purpose-why-it-matters-to-your-life-and-business/.

If you have connected with your purpose, write it below. Once you pen your purpose, you can skip to section three or review the rest of this section as a refresher.

My purpose is _____

_____

_____

_____

_____

If you are not ready to fill in the field above, keep reading to explore what you were created to do. Let's start with a simple question. What do you do for others that makes you feel accomplished? Sit with this question for a minute before you read on. Think through those times you felt elated serving others. What were you doing? If you can't think of anything, recall when you felt happy. What was happening? Be sure to write down your thoughts so you can refer back to them later. If you remember more than one type of example, collect them all on a document.

Here are some illustrations to get your thoughts churning. Some people like to teach others and enjoy seeing the light bulb switch on when they finally get it. Some like to help others find jobs and feel a sense of meaning when they see others develop in their role. Some like to take a project from the ground up and watch it flourish. Others like planting financial seeds and hearing reports on how that donation provided relief or opened up opportunities.

Several experiences may come to mind. Grab a pen and paper and start a list. If you are having trouble, reach out to a family member or friend to ask when you seemed most happy interacting with others. Feel free to write down more than one thought. Take it a step further and test out some of these theories. See what brings you joy, then come back and analyze your research. This exercise may not be a one-time magic bullet in finding purpose, but it will definitely open your eyes to relevant trends. It took me years to figure out I wanted to be a part of helping families thrive. It kept coming back to my thoughts each time I volunteered for a cause or envisioned what I wanted to see happen over my lifespan. I finally took it to heart and started running with it. Starting with my own family, my goal is to elevate each member with the tools needed to soar spiritually, mentally, and financially.

Section 2 – Core Values

Identifying your core values will also help direct your path. Personal core values are traits or principles you strongly believe in that help define who you are. Integrity, kindness, honesty, and financial security are typical examples of personal core values. Core values are also described as character traits. For instance, someone known for always doing the right thing likely values integrity. Hundreds of core values represent personal beliefs.

Scienceofpeople.com[24] includes a collection of 216 core values to choose from. The list consists of attributes like honesty, integrity, confidence, promise-keeper, and self-love. Visit the website to view the entire collection of core values, or search other websites to find more options. Then, choose the top three to five value words that resonate most with you. It may be not easy to choose just five from such an

---

24   Hailey, Logan. "Core Values List: The Only 216 Values You'll Ever Need." Science of People, September 22, 2022. https://www.scienceofpeople.com/core-values/.

extensive list. If this is the case for you, try this exercise. Start with circling all the core values that are important to you, then whittle your selection down to ten. Next, start the introspective task of choosing your top three to five.

Write your top three to five core values here:

_____

_____

_____

_____

_____

Section 3 – Mission

Now that you know what activities give you a sense of accomplishment and have chosen three to five top core values that resonate most with you, let's merge these two to unveil your mission.

Let's say you feel most accomplished when working with small children. You love to hear the giggles when you play with them or hear them parrot a word back to you when reading with them. And you've decided trust, honor, cleanliness, playfulness, and teamwork are your core values. If you merge those, you may find that your purpose could be assisting children with a safe, clean place to learn and play. This mission is broad enough for you to get involved in many ways to advocate for children, but it also narrows your scope so you are not spending time on activities that are not meaningful to you.

Try this on your own. Review the activities you've written down that make you feel accomplished, combine them with your core values, and start crafting a statement that truly aligns with you. It may take several iterations, but keep trying until your words feel comfortable and represent what you want.

Before I take on these types of assignments, I envision myself as having already achieved my goal. For instance, I close my eyes and imagine I'm at the top of my game, fulfilling my purpose. I see myself in a crowd of people being applauded or patted on the back for reaching a goal well beyond what I planned as I satisfy a significant need. In my specific case, my goal looks like this: I have inspired and coached a husband, wife, and their children to pivot from day-to-day survival to planning each quarter together; they receive rewards of prosperity, strong bonds, and love throughout the process. Each step brings more and more family success. Parents are modeling healthy relationships for their kids. The family communicates with each other on a daily basis, and they are all upstanding members of the community, contributing to the health of the human ecosystem.

I would like you to try this, too. Close your eyes and envision your ideal self at the top of your game. How does it look? What are you doing? How are others reacting? How does it feel? Write this down in your journal.

A personal mission statement is:
1. A tool for making difficult decisions.
2. A framework for how you want to live your life and express your mission.
3. A beacon to those around you about the kind of person you are.

4. A declaration that motivates and inspires you to stay the course.
5. A statement of your values and life priorities.[25]

Many visionaries, planning experts, and career executives suggest posting your life's mission statement in a place you can see daily. I highly recommend writing your mission statement and placing it in your closet, bathroom, or office—a place you often occupy. This will help remind you of your goals and your commitment to yourself.

Below are a few life mission statements from the Indeed Career Guide at Indeed.com. Reviewing other people's life mission statements as you polish yours may be helpful. Before you read them, though, I suggest that you try writing your own first. At this infancy stage, you don't want to mix other people's core thoughts and goals with your own. You want to stay as authentic to yourself as possible. So, try writing your own goal before reviewing the declarations below.

Draft Mission Statement _____

_____

_____

_____

---

[25] Davenport, Barrie. "How to Write a Personal Mission Statement (And 28 Mission Statement Examples)." Live Bold and Bloom, May 1, 2023. https://live-boldandbloom.com/05/passion-in-life/personal-mission-statement.

Examples of Life Mission Statements[26]

"To use my writing skills to inspire and educate others around the world to make a change."

"To use my gifts as a speaker to improve the self-worth of people around the world."

"To inspire children to be more than they thought they could be."

"To thrive in my journey through life and learn life's lessons along the way."

"To help men, women, and children find hope after loss."

"To create innovative technology solutions that will improve people's lives around the globe."

"To equip others with the tools and resources to pursue the life they want to live."

"To give students the resources and attention they need to grow into confident, effective adults."

"To create stories that educate, entertain, and inspire people worldwide."

---

26 Herrity, Jennifer. "How to Write a Personal Mission Statement (40 Examples." Indeed, July 31, 2023. https://www.indeed.com/career-advice/career-development/personal-mission-statement-examples.

> *"To use my gifts to improve the self-worth and wealth of women around the world."*
>
> *"To be a source of hope by offering humility, optimism, and support to everyone I meet."*
>
> *"To leave the world a better place than I found it."*

As you can see, mission statements do not have to be long, drawn-out descriptions. They just need one or two sentences that energize and help you maintain your focus. Keeping them simple and broad allows you to accomplish several things that would fit into your mission bucket, giving you room for further impact and, therefore, a more successful legacy. But if you are someone who is easily led off track, add some guardrails in your language. For instance, if you strongly desire to work in the mental health space, instead of stating, "To leave the earth better than I found it," you could commit "to leave mental health education better than I found it." That simple change could keep you grounded in your mission.

Chapter 15:

Planning

Have you heard the saying, "Fail to plan; plan to fail"? Planning is important in every consequential endeavor you take on. Your legacy is no different.

By now, you should understand what moves you. You have uncovered your top core values and have a written mission statement that reflects your authentic self. You are getting closer to activating legacy living. Creating a plan is the next critical step to bringing your legacy goals alive. Legacy thinking is a good place to begin.

Legacy thinking is a model that starts with considering the end of your goal first. It's planning using a backward design. Identify the long-term impact you want to make, then analyze the actions you need to take to reach that point.[27] For example, you have a goal of teaming up with a local food bank to feed the hungry for two weeks in November: before, during, and after Thanksgiving. Using legacy thinking, you first look at your endpoint: delivering 500 turkeys, 250 hams, 200 pounds of dressing, green beans, sweet potatoes, and 100 pounds of gravy to the food bank at 7 a.m. Monday, November 10. Next, you start adding activities to your timeline, working backwards from your goal date, like:

---

27   Mind Tools Content Team. "What Is Legacy Thinking?" MindTools. Accessed October 5, 2023. https://www.mindtools.com/a3axrm1/what-is-legacy-thinking.

- Scheduling a diesel trunk to pick up and deliver a refrigerated container with food items to the food bank on Sunday, November 9.
- Scheduling and hosting a food drive collecting money and canned goods, November 7–9, at a nearby grocery store.
- Soliciting grocery stores to provide space for November 7–9 and donations by October 31.
- Advertising on social media from October 1–November 9 and sending press releases to all listed news organizations.
- Creating a press release to send to news organizations for publicity on October 1.

Get the gist? Keeping the end in mind enables you to work toward your objective in sequence, step by step, rather than considering those tasks retrospectively. The most important benefit of legacy thinking is that it brings purpose to your activities and places your actions in a clearer context. Knowing that you're building something to last will make you more focused, motivated, empowered, and satisfied.

Legacy thinking can also be used in other goal-oriented areas in your life. Try employing legacy thinking with other areas of your life that aren't part of your legacy plan, like a work project. It will strengthen your procedures and make you a more organized leader.[28]

Planning Worksheet

Below are two worksheet examples that will help you keep track of the objectives you want to accomplish. One table only lists goals. The second table uses the legacy thinking model to complete your goals. The point is to keep a written reminder of your specific goals and include

---

28   Mind Tools Content Team. (n.d.). "What Is Legacy Thinking? Beginning With the End in Mind." MindTools. https://www.mindtools.com/a3axrm1/what-is-legacy-thinking.

the steps to get there. The charts also have space for time parameters and a description of the end goals. Writing these details with a deadline is not a pressure tactic; it's just a guideline to keep you centered if your mind goes off track. You can use these tables as is or customize them to best serve your needs.

Although the first worksheet includes legacy goals, remember that this plan is for the life you are living today. Be sure to make the tasks realistic and doable. This worksheet can be as intricate or as simple as you like.

I set simple guidelines because I get overwhelmed as I overthink things or give myself too many tasks. I include just four essential components:

1. Make sure my goals are measurable—this helps determine if I have successfully reached them.
2. Include the **why** behind my goals—this keeps me motivated.
3. List tactics/steps—these keep me moving forward; they can always be revised and updated.
4. A timeline is extremely important—it keeps me from procrastinating. I also like to add a column for notes in case I need to provide additional details or reminders. See Table 1 below.

Goals	Why	Steps	Timeline	Notes
Create living will	Provide family guidance in case I'm disabled	Use online template; tell husband and daughters where to find copy of LW	Begin by Feb. 14 Complete by March 14	Review and update LW annually
Join the Assist 4 Life Foundation advisory board	Enhance number of scholarships for women in construction	Write down ideas; reach out to Assist 4 Life; join board or participate as volunteer	March 1	
Volunteer at church	Further goal of being a servant leader	Ask church where they need volunteers the most; sync schedule and join	April 1	
Donate to college scholarship	Advance life mission of supporting families of color	Research college fund scholarships to align with my beliefs	Ongoing quarterly donations starting in Jan	Donate 20% of my company bonus

Create family tree book	To pass on family accomplishments and details to future generations	Gather pictures and family background; check with elders for accuracy	Begin May 1 Complete by Dec. 20	Make several copies and send to each maternal grandchild
Review and update existing will	Make sure newly acquired valuables are added to will	As I require	Ongoing	

Table 2 consists of one of my goals and step-by-step actions using legacy thinking or backward planning. Once I list all my goals, I involve legacy thinking to design a gradual workflow for each intention. Work upward on your list, adding as many lines as needed to reach the goal.

GOAL: Create Living Will by March 14	
Feb. 14	Find free living will template online to use
Feb. 28	Fill out the template while making decisions on health circumstances
Feb. 28	Choose an executor and let them know of their responsibility
March 3	Find a notary and officialize the document
March 10	Let other family members know this exists
March 14	All tasks for living will completed

Your spreadsheets should be a living document. Update it, write on it, revise it, and check it often. Create calendar alerts to remind yourself to revisit them. I still like to print goals on paper versus just keeping them on my phone or computer. I place this along with my mission in a visible spot, like on the wall in my workspace, so I am constantly reminded of what I want to accomplish. For me, it's out of sight, out of mind. If I don't see my goals often, I forget to work toward them daily or weekly.

Planning is also critical when leaving tangible items to your loved ones. Heartprint legacy goals take longer and could easily derail if you don't have a detailed plan to keep yourself engaged. Having an exhaustive list of physical properties is just as critical.

Too often, I have seen family members struggle with organizing or clearing an estate after a loved one has passed. On top of all the grief, heartache, and stress that comes with losing someone, family members are tasked with figuring out the deceased's wishes and intentions, or dividing sentimental assets or items. I remember when one of my friend's grandparents passed away, and her aunts and uncle fought over a beautifully carved grandfather clock. The statuesque wooden timepiece was a prized possession of her grandparents, and everyone adored it. Siblings stopped talking to each other as they disputed their birthright and rankings over the clock. The oldest thought it was only logical that she should have it. The youngest, who cared for her grandmother until the end, thought she should get it. And, the son, who often pitched in financially, thought his direct family deserved it. It was a mess. I never found out who got the clock. However, I remember the family fighting was so stressful that the grandchildren suffered from the lost and damaged relationships. It really doesn't matter who won the battle; the actual impact was the strained and severed connections from the battle.

Do your family a favor and dignify them with a detailed description of how you want your possessions divided. This way, instead of family members facing off against each other, they can blame ill feelings on you, which will quickly fade because you're not there to argue with them. This parting act could be a determining factor for fractured sibling relationships or a strong, successful family bond. We discuss taking account of your personal items again in the upcoming Last Will and Testament section. This topic is important enough to mention twice.

Consider making your own funeral plans once you put your affairs in order. It feels weird to think about your death, but ignoring it won't make it go away. We are going to die one day. This is the circle of life. If you are a Christ-follower, take comfort in knowing this earthly phase is not the end for us. *"For God so loved the world that he gave his one and only Son, that whoever believes in him shall not perish but have eternal life"* (John 3:16 NIV). Believers will live on with our Father in heaven. So, don't shy away from planning your funeral; it will take a load off of your loved ones remaining here on earth.

Planning your celebration of life ceremony may initially feel overwhelming, but once you dive into the details, it becomes easier, like any other legacy planning task. Take it one step at a time using legacy thinking—starting with the end in mind. Think about your vision for your memorial services and write it down as your end goal. If you would like an hour-long observance full of your favorite things, start from there. For instance, if you want a special song played on the piano, a favorite Scripture or poem read aloud, or certain kinds of flowers you love, add that to your list. Then, learn about the funeral process and start planning. Here are some simple steps from US Urn Online, a website that provides service information on funerals and products.[29]

---

29 "How to Plan a Funeral: Simple Memorial Planning Steps." US Urns

Educate Yourself and Plan Everything You Can in Advance
This will ease stress on your loved ones, reduce costs, and help you get what you want.

Research information online and tap into local funeral directors to ask questions.

Set Your Funeral Budget
Funerals can be expensive. However, there are many ways to save on costs as you consider affordable versus high-end options. Create a funeral budget by:
- Researching the average cost of a funeral
- Looking at your finances and funeral insurance, then determining what you can afford
- Considering accepting donations in lieu of flowers
- Asking a friend to help you stay on task and avoid unnecessary purchases

Funeral homes require payment upfront via cash, check, or credit card. Be prepared to pay for your arrangements or set up a payment plan. Also, consider life insurance or prepaid funeral plans to help pay costs. A prepaid funeral plan is an insurance policy through a funeral home of your choosing that helps pay for funeral costs.

Choose Disposition Method
Would you prefer a burial or cremation? There is a lot of information online on the disposition methods, such as cremation or burial. Do your research, then make your decision. It's not a bad idea to discuss this with close family as well. Some family members may have strong opinions.

Online. Accessed October 6, 2023. https://www.usurnsonline.com/funerals.

Choose the Type of Service

There are many types of funeral services, including the "before" events (wake, viewing, visitation) as well as "after" events (reception, cremation, scattering, graveside service).

For most people, the primary decision is between a traditional funeral or a less formal, more contemporary celebration of life ceremony, which is more of a memorial service.

Plan the Service Events

After choosing what event should make up the service through the ceremony's flow and what should be included, find an officiant and provide details on the readings, Scriptures, prayers, and songs. Other things to consider are open versus closed casket, open mic sharing time, or other special memorial tributes.

Plan a Reception

What will people do after the service? Many ceremonies have a repass following the eulogy or burial. This is where guests can sit down and share a meal. It allows family and friends more time to fellowship and comfort each other.

Choose a Final Resting Place

Lastly, choose a resting place. Some people prefer to have their body interred in a crypt or mausoleum, which could add a sizable amount to your budget. Most people choose a traditional cemetery plot with a grave marker. If you choose cremation, your final resting place can vary significantly. The family could scatter all or part of your ashes in a particular place. Loved ones could keep the cremation urn at home. You could have your urn buried or placed in a funeral home niche. Be sure to document your final wishes.

If you still struggle to make decisions for your funeral, solicit a friend or close family member to help you manage the tougher parts of your planning.

The overall aim of thoughtfully planning your life, even the end of it, is to enlarge your success rate of a positive legacy by providing uncomplicated gifts of stability, peace, and protection. The benefit to your lineage decreases the propensity for bickering and increases opportunities for growth and healthy relationships. The benefit to society would be bequeathing a lasting positive impact that would elevate future generations.

Chapter 16:
Action

It is never too early or too late to start working on your legacy seriously. Wherever you are in life—old, young, rich, poor, married, divorced, working or not—you can find ways to leave a positive mark and touch someone's life meaningfully. The fact that you are reading this book is a strong indicator that you are ready to begin or continue the journey. So, give yourself a high-five. The earlier you start, the more opportunities you have to make mistakes, learn from them, and start again. But even if you have waited until later in life, you still have time to create something special. As long as you are breathing and of sound mind, you can produce a generational impact on your family and the world.

Although more than half of adults in the U.S. feel leaving a legacy is the right thing to do, only 33 percent have documented their end-of-life arrangements, like wills and estate plans, according to legalzoo.com. Only 30 to 40 percent of households receive some inheritance, yet an older survey reveals some of our wealth transfer has been unintentional. Inheritances reflect a mixture of intentional and accidental bequests, with the latter twice as prevalent.[30] Some families were lucky to receive a gift because their ancestors did not specifically assign them to it.

---

30   Wolff, Edward N., and Maur Gittleman. "Inheritances and the Distribution of Wealth or Whatever Happened to the Great Inheritance Boom?" U.S. Bureau of Labor Statistics, January 2011. https://www.bls.gov/osmr/research-papers/2011/pdf/ec110030.pdf.

This highlights the importance of getting your affairs in order as early as possible. You never know what life has planned for you, and it's always better to prepare for the unknown rather than ignore its inevitability.

The COVID-19 pandemic serves as a prominent example of preparing for the unknown. Who would have ever guessed a deadly virus would sweep through every nation, taking thousands of lives and making even more painfully ill? Globally, 6,947,192 people lost their lives to COVID-19, according to the World Health Organization's numbers from January 2020 to January 2023. The United States tops the chart of countries with the most deaths:

1. America—2,956,943
2. Europe—2,243,097
3. Southeast Asia—806,441

In the wake of that devastation, people took action. Forty-one percent of Americans with loved ones who had a serious case of COVID-19 created a will compared to 29 percent who had no close experiences with severe COVID-19. Americans who dealt with a serious bout of COVID-19 themselves are now 66 percent more likely to have a will than not, according to a 2022 Estate Planning Study by Caring.com.

If you worked through the activities in the last three chapters, you should have a solid outline of the legacy you will leave and a route to get there. Now, when or how do you take your first step? This may sound like a no-brainer to some, but others can get paralysis through analysis—stuck working out every detail, trying to make it perfect before they take the first step. They often never start the process because they've worked themselves into a frenzy trying to ensure the plan is foolproof, or they burn themselves out overthinking. But a plan on paper is only that. So, don't stop there. A written outline is just a page full of words until it's coupled with action.

Remember Thomas Edison's quote, "Genius is 1 percent inspiration and 99 percent perspiration." A plan is a tiny portion of what generates success. Words put into action is the sweet spot. Plus, procrastination and delaying action can lead to missed opportunities and regrets. Don't wait until your plan on paper is perfect or you've addressed every angle or crisis that could appear. Move forward with action sooner rather than later. Once you get that ball rolling, the momentum will take hold, and goals are met before you know it.

Some procrastinate because they prioritize other interests, and others hesitate to take the first step because they are too nervous. The plan sounded good when they were creating it. Now that it's time to execute, the proposal may appear too lofty, or they think others will not take it seriously. Just remember, everyone who has stepped out of their comfort zone and set out to do something novel or big has experienced some nervousness. It's absolutely natural and a common emotion. It's so typical that mental health experts have thought through steps to overcome it. Here are seven tips from Eugene Therapy to get past the jitters to move forward regardless of temporary angst:

1. Acknowledge your nervousness.
   Recognize that it's normal to feel nervous and okay to feel this way.

2. Challenge your anxious thoughts.
   Consider the best and worst-case scenarios, then consider what is truly realistic. While uncertainty plays a big part in nervousness, make peace with not knowing what could happen and vow to be okay regardless of what happens.

3. Talk to someone.
   Speak to a trusted loved one. They could be a source of comfort and help you think through your ideas.

4. Break it down.
   Break down the task or goal into smaller, more manageable steps. This can help you feel less overwhelmed and more in control.

5. Visualize success.
   Imagine yourself completing the task or achieving your goal. This can help you feel more confident.

6. Take action.
   Start with the small task and gradually work your way up. This can help you build momentum.

7. Practice self-care.
   Take care of yourself by getting enough sleep, eating healthy, and doing things that help you relax and decrease stress. Practice relaxation by taking deep breaths.[31]

The first steps can be scary, but it's also the first move toward achieving satisfying goals. Just keep moving forward, even if you are nervous. You'll soon replace those anxious thoughts with feelings of accomplishment and success. Just push yourself out there. It's okay to start with something small or not so intimidating. You may dream of impacting the world, the community, or your family. Feel free to dip your toe before diving in head first.

Let's say you want to write a book about your forefathers and align their legacies with the generations they have impacted today. This vision would take a ton of research, including combing through

---

31   Zola, Marc. "5 Tips to Manage Anticipatory Anxiety." Eugene Therapy, October 12, 2021. https://eugenetherapy.com/article/5-tips-to-manage-anticipatory-anxiety.

courthouse records, searching through national archives and coroner files, accessing repositories of microfilm and catalogs in a library, and visiting all the elders and family historians within the clan. It's a mammoth task if you look at the whole picture of your goal.

However, if you chop the project into smaller tasks, you can accomplish your vision more easily while assembling notable pieces along the way. Instead of jumping right into the intergenerational publication, you could start by collecting stories and pictures from your elders. Collate them and you'll already have a small historical book you could share with the family. This relic alone could be passed down through generations to provide family awareness. Next, choose one ascendent to research. Uncover more of your family's background through court records and other documents to add facts and substance to those stories. Then, choose the next forefather to focus on and repeat. This example illustrates baby steps that lead to larger ones. In essence, start small so you don't feel overwhelmed. Allow yourself to work your way into the more complicated tasks of your project. It will feel less intimidating and, in turn, make it easier to take that first step.

Here's a personal real-life example. I believe my life's purpose is to elevate and advance families of color. My vision is vast enough to accomplish a diverse number of things, but it also has guardrails to keep me aligned with my focus. For instance, if there is an opportunity for me to invest time into building a clean, loving facility for injured and abused animals, I may respectfully decline. While this is certainly a worthy cause that needs attention, it could hinder immersion in my ultimate goal: building up family units. However, if there is a request for my energy to support counseling efforts to help emotionally withdrawn mothers and fathers, I am more likely to join the cause. It aligns with my goals.

My mission has led me to co-author a book called *We Got This Sis* with a friend who has strong family values and loves to take on projects to help the community. Our collaboration focuses on empowering women to be their best selves for their families, friends, and communities. It started with a collection of relatable stories for a book and led to speaking engagements and additional collaboration opportunities. I realized how much I enjoyed encouraging others and decided to explore this side of my talents more. I enrolled in life coaching classes and desired to zero in on the importance of leaving a legacy. Now I'm a certified life coach specializing in legacy planning, supporting individuals and families who want to leave a positive impact.

Staying focused is also essential when taking the first steps. I had several false starts because I allowed small distractions to pull my attention away from my big goal. Staying in tune with my vision finally led to accomplishing my objectives. If we allow ourselves to get off track, it will take longer to reach our end goal, or, heaven forbid, we may never make it there at all. Stay vigilant and dismiss anything that would encourage you to detour. We discuss the importance of staying on track in Chapter 19, *Course Correction*.

I can't say this enough: if you think you have tons of time to get started on your legacy plan, remember that time is not promised to anyone. The longer you wait to take action, the less time you have to achieve your goals. Starting now will allow you to make the most of your time and increase your chances of success. It also gives you time to learn from your experiences and mistakes. The sooner you start, the sooner you know what works and what doesn't, allowing you to adjust your approach accordingly. By starting today, you give yourself more time to reach fulfillment.

Part 5
Care

It's very important that people know that I really enjoy everything that has happened to me. And I tell my kids ... you're not going to be the tallest, fastest, prettiest, the best track runner, but you can be the nicest human being that someone has ever met in their life. And I just want to leave that legacy that being nice is a true treasure.

—George Foreman, *boxer and businessman*

Chapter 17:
Motivation

We are hard-wired to leave a significant inheritance.

A *Psychology Today* article called "The Animal Urge to Leave a Legacy: Planting Seeds Stimulates Your Happy Chemicals" explains that our brain focuses on our legacy without conscious intent because it gives us a happy high. The neurochemistry that drives animals to promote their genes is what drives you to care about your legacy. The mammalian limbic system releases a surge of happiness when you do things that promote reproductive success. Animals focus on the survival of their DNA without conscious intent, thanks to natural selection. "Animals just do things that stimulate their happy chemicals and avoid their icky chemicals," said Loretta G. Breuning, Ph.D., author of the article. Just think about how you feel when you show kindness toward someone, especially a family member. I get all gushy when I see my kids' smiles when I bring home a special box of cupcakes. Something about doing nice and unexpected things puts me in a good mood. We all desire that feeling of elation and gravitate towards good deeds for our loved ones because it makes us feel good.

While we may not live to see our seed fully blossom, it helps when we realize society has good things today because people before us planted seeds. Think of Gregor Mendel, who discovered genetics. No one realized his genius until 20 years after he died. Mendel worked in obscure isolation, then planted his self-published book in monasteries throughout Europe. One copy eventually inspired later scientists.[32] Today, genetics is part of every medical consideration as we continue to build on Mendel's findings. If people only planted when they were sure of seeing fruit, all the good in the world today would not exist. So, keep planting even if you only see the roots.

How do we stay stimulated to plant and fertilize even when we don't see results? The answer could be as simple as identifying our true motivation. Connecting to what inspires us, the reason we have committed to giving, will keep us on track and engaged. The key here is taking time to uncover the impetus for our goals. Strong legacies are created when we are in touch with our authentic selves, understanding what ignites us and marrying that with a planned goal.

Here's an example: if you want a certain lifestyle, you probably try to find a reasonable way to get it. Let's say your vehicle to that lifestyle is working Monday through Friday, laboring 10 to 12 hours per day to fund your way of living. If you are passionate about that position, you can do that for a while. But, if you don't understand what's influencing you, you could dread work and quit your job. The long hours could overshadow the hope for this lifestyle.

Conversely, what if you fully know what fuels you to work for that lifestyle? What if the lifestyle meant better schools for your children, a safer neighborhood for your family, or a chance to give your parents ownership of a home, something they've always wanted? When you think about going to work, you'll picture the faces of those you work for. You will be constantly reminded of your "why." You are less likely to give up! The goal is the lifestyle. The paycheck is the means to

---

32 Breuning, Ph.D., Loretta G. "The Animal Urge to Leave a Legacy: Planting Seeds Stimulates Your Happy Chemicals." *Psychology Today*, August 2, 2011. https://www.psychologytoday.com/us/blog/your-neurochemical-self/201108/the-animal-urge-leave-legacy.

achieve it. And, your motivation is a better way of life for your children, spouse, or parents.

This same concept should apply to your specific legacy goals. Your impactful legacy is the prize. Planning and execution are the vehicles to get there. It's up to you to uncover your motivation. While your inspiration may seem extremely obvious, you may be surprised how many of us are disconnected from what drives us. True catalysts are sometimes hidden in past experiences, like a river flowing down a mountain; the hidden rocks determine the water's currents. Take the time to pinpoint your genuine motivation. It could be an opportunity to turn something negative into a positive.

My motivation comes from many personal and sometimes conflicting experiences growing up in a middle-class community in northwest Houston. I will start by sharing my parents' childhood background for a better understanding. My mother and father grew up in a socio-economic class familiar to many Black people in the 1940s. Growing up in wooded pastures in Haynesville, Louisiana, my mom admits to being dirt poor with 12 siblings. My mother's father passed away from heart failure when she was around six years old—leaving my grandmother, Ola Mae Wilson, to raise 13 kids off the land her parents left her and her nine siblings. Picking cotton to pay bills and tending to their garden was their morning, evening, and weekend ritual.

My father felt his family was well off compared to others in their small country town outside of Jasper, Texas. The Bluiett family ran a farm with horses, cows, pigs, and chickens and planted corn, peas, and tomatoes. My father grew up with both parents and often reminisces about his father working as a logger and tending the fields of property he inherited from his parents. My father's mother kept the house, preparing hot meals just in time for Grandpa to sit at the dinner table. My dad had four brothers and four sisters, all with important duties around their farm. The Bluiett family had a working patriarch, owned acres of land, and traded livestock.

On the other hand, my mom's family, the Wilsons, were raised mainly by a single mother because their father passed away at an early age. They picked cotton and cultivated other people's land for currency. This exemplifies why my father believes he was better off growing up than many rural homesteads. He felt his family had a certain level of control over their financial fate that he recognized others did not have. Nevertheless, when my father left home, he found himself in the same economic position as other poor kids who had to work for every penny to get on his feet. Grandpa Charles Westmoreland and MoMo Lodie Bell Simmons Bluiett lived the good life compared to others in their community, but they were far from wealthy. They had no resources to send my dad into the world with a monetary cushion. I remember my dad's stories of using hair grease to cook birds he caught on the Prairie View A&M campus for a meal. I don't know how true that is, but he gave us kids a vivid example of his struggles.

Once my parents married, they merged their salaries to make a better life for themselves and our family. Right before the fourth grade, I remember moving from a lower middle-class neighborhood to one where two-story houses were a dime a dozen and a golf course sprawled throughout. I was young, but I still remember the feeling of accomplishment, especially when my cousin visited our new two-story home. One claimed he got lost because our house was as big as the Astrodome. It was less than 3,000 square feet, but it was a mansion to us. My mom said we left the old neighborhood because the schools were better and the crime rate was lower in the new one. We were moving up, surviving in northwest Houston on a well-thought-out budget.

I couldn't help but notice, however, that the white residents in the area were beyond surviving. They seemed to be thriving. Once I entered high school, I discovered some students were going to Hawaii and Europe for vacation. When some of my friends turned 16, they got new cars. There were even a couple of BMWs in the school parking lot. While cars and houses are only a symbol of success (we don't know if bank accounts were stretched to get these luxury items), it spotlighted the ancillary income to which these families had access. They had enough to spend on pleasurable things. They were not limited to the necessities.

I was at a loss when I heard the stories of grandparents, uncles, or aunts who bought cars or paid for expensive golf lessons for their families. How could grandparents afford all these costly things? My grandparents only gave us a quarter for candy or baked a special cake for a birthday. Why would uncles and aunts spend their hard-earned money on nieces and nephews? Weren't they concerned about their own immediate families? One high schooler got a new car from his grandparents because he was promised a nice vehicle on his 16th birthday if he made all As and Bs on his report card. Another family traveled to Hawaii on their grandparents' dime. To get the whole family together each year, another student's grandparents would plan and pay for an exotic trip. One student had to play a sport and learn an instrument to comply with the terms of his trust fund. I did not know it then, but inheritance and legacy were the deep pockets and driving force behind these enviable luxuries.

In hindsight, witnessing these marvels from the outside left a window of hope in my spirit. While my parents gave us children a life they never had, I was still jealous of my high school friends and coveted what they had. My parents exposed us to more than a good education and a life without crime. They opened up a whole new way of life that many in our clan never knew existed. Because of that, I want to usher in a better life for my loved ones. I want to have and provide the same conveniences and luxuries to my children and grandchildren that I witnessed in my old neighborhood.

Things get done when you are highly motivated. Tap into what inspires you. If it happens to be something unpleasant from your past, don't run from it. Face it. Find a positive way to turn it around and reframe it. Use it to fuel something good. Let that boost your legacy plan.

Chapter 18:
Who to Give To?

Leaving a contribution is a right. Receiving a contribution is a privilege.

As a donor, you have complete control over who receives your valuables once you pass away, provided you have legally designated your assets. If you have children, other loved ones, or a cause near and dear to your heart, you may want to gift them a financial windfall or other valuable resources. But, giving away your treasures can cause concern, especially when considering some of the pitfalls that accompany leaving a monetary inheritance. When choosing your heirs, it's crucial to ensure they are equipped to handle what is being left to them.

If you plan to leave something behind for your family, you may face the reality that some relatives make responsible financial decisions, and others do not. Can you leave those irresponsible members out of the will? Is it okay to leave some descendants more assets than others? For those of us without biological children, should we leave it all to our step-children, nieces, and nephews, or someone who will care for us during our elder years? Is it okay not to leave anything to family but give it all to worthy causes that will help others in the community or worldwide? These are all valid questions, and the answer is yes to all of them. You can do what you want because you determine who receives your valuables. However, you should do your homework to make an informed decision.

To help, let's explore different angles. First, review the eye-opening statistics listed below from various financial institutions and experts;

then, we will look at a few ways to work around serial challenges plaguing inherited money. At the end of this chapter, you will have an opportunity to connect prospective resources, not just money, with potential heirs. Once you finish, you should have the tools to enrich your family and other heirs for future generations.

Before we jump into the stats, please note that weighty words like "generational wealth" and riches mentioned throughout this chapter and the rest of the book may seem like giant, intimidating references to those of us who don't have millions of dollars in the bank. For this project, I ask that you consider generational wealth as assets passed down from generation to generation, including money, resources, and other forms of affluence. Envision your valuables as the wealth mentioned here—intergenerational riches that can be used to build financial security for future generations despite your economic class. Hearts & Wallets' research shows that inheritances are now expanding beyond those belonging to high-net-worth households. Fifty-four percent of U.S. households with less than $100,000 in investable assets expect to receive or leave inheritances as of 2022, a 15 percent increase from 2015. Most of these households have no prior experience with inheritances.[33] So, do not get discouraged by the popular reference to generational wealth; be encouraged because you are working your way to taking care of your family and leaving a long-lasting legacy of love.

Here are some statistics about inheritance:
- Fifty-five percent of Millennials say it's a parent's obligation to leave an inheritance, while only 36 percent of Boomers (the generation most of their parents belong to) agree, according to Merrill Lynch, a wealth management institution.

---

33   Cagnassola, Mary Ellen. "More Americans Are Leaving Inheritances—And It's Not Just Wealthy People." Money, April 12, 2023. https://money.com/more-americans-leaving-inheritances.

- Only 9.5 percent of individuals with parents without a college degree expect an inheritance, while 23.6 percent of individuals who have parents with a degree expect to receive bequeathed assets (annuity.org).
- A study over 20 years revealed that almost 70 percent of families lose a portion of their inheritance due to fighting over the estate they are inheriting. Some legal advisors point out that the battles are not always about money. Often, items such as jewelry or another heirloom can be in the middle of a contested battle between heirs.[34]
- "Looking at the numbers, 78 percent of grantors feel the next generation is not financially responsible enough to handle inheritance," says Chris Heilmann, U.S. Trust's chief fiduciary executive.[35]
- "It takes the average recipient of an inheritance 19 days until they buy a new car."[36]
- According to the Global Credit Union, most people use inherited money to save or create an emergency savings fund, to pay down debts such as credit cards, personal or student loans, or vehicle loans, or to build a college fund.
- Seventy percent of generational wealth doesn't make it past the second generation, and 90 percent disappears by the third.[37]
- Top five reasons generational wealth is lost:
    1. Lack of financial literacy
    2. Inheritance and estate planning issues
    3. Lifestyle inflation and overspending

---

34   DuPage County Divorce Lawyers | Illinois. Accessed October 6, 2023. https://www.dupagelawyers.com.
35   Taylor, Chris. "70% of Rich Families Lose Their Wealth by the Second Generation." Money, June 17, 2015. https://money.com/rich-families-lose-wealth.
36   Ibid.
37   Ibid.

4. Lack of asset diversification
5. Socio-economic factors (systemic racism and income inequality)[38]

- According to a survey conducted by the Federal Reserve, between 2016 and 2019, the average inheritance received in the U.S. was $46,200. The average for the wealthiest 1 percent of individuals surveyed was $719,000, while the average for the bottom 50 percent was only $9,700.
- If you do not leave a will, the line of inheritance begins with direct offspring, starting with your children, then your grandchildren, followed by any great-grandchildren, and so on. The legal status of stepchildren and adopted children varies by jurisdiction.[39]
- Without a will, probate court will allow children to inherit equal shares. Predeceased children are represented by their own descendants (inheritance by representation). No distinction is made between children born in and out of wedlock. They are all equal under inheritance law.[40]
- Large inheritances vary considerably, but it's safe to say that anything over $100,000 falls into this category.[41]

Pretty interesting research, right? The numbers above give you things to consider when choosing your heirs. Just know whatever you decide, there are experts who can assist.

---

38   The Builders at Wealth Factory. "Why Is Generational Wealth Lost? Top 5 Reasons Explained." Wealth Factory, May 4, 2023. https://wealthfactory.com/articles/why-is-generational-wealth-lost.
39   Investopedia. Accessed October 6, 2023. https://www.investopedia.com.
40   My-Life.LU, Aug 21, 2017
41   Chatterton & Associates. Accessed October 6, 2023. https://chatterton-inc.com/

Since one of the biggest concerns about leaving a financial inheritance is that heirs will quickly and frivolously spend the money, many professionals, books, and articles are available to prepare you and your heirs to manage funds with control. Here are some examples of advice you may receive:

- Money advisors suggest giving your kids and grandkids a crash course in financial literacy. Many financial institutions provide specialized learning materials and courses to get heirs up to speed. If you can teach your heirs smart money lessons, you have pushed family wealth forward another 30 to 40 years.[42]
- Give your heirs a financial roadmap in the form of a family mission statement, advises the U.S. Trust. You can lay out what you expect regarding spending, saving, and giving back, as well as pass along strategies for building wealth.
- You can develop a trust that controls the amount and timing of dispersed funds.
- Develop rules for receivers, like an heir must pursue a college degree and hold a professional career to receive funds from a trust.

In essence, where there is a will, there is a way. Start now preparing your heirs to manage their inheritance.

Another important way to ensure heirs are prepared for their incoming estate is to be transparent with them. Fifty-two percent of people don't know where their parents store estate planning documents, according to LegalZoom.com. Whomever and why you decide to give should not be a secret. "Parents and grandparents should communicate the whats and whys of their will in a group setting, with all their children present, long before the will is read," says David Mullins, a

---

42   Taylor, Chris. "70% of Rich Families Lose Their Wealth by the Second Generation." Money, June 17, 2015. https://money.com/rich-families-lose-wealth.

planner in Richlands, Virginia.[43] In this group setting, you can discuss problems as a family beforehand. It's better to do this when the patriarch and/or matriarch are around to explain or make adjustments than wait until they are gone and their desires are misunderstood. "Trust me, siblings will find out who got what," says Mullins. "Without proper communication, this can destroy families."

While most leave an endowment for their direct descendants, other potential heirs exist besides an ascendant's biological and adopted children. Spouses, grandchildren, nieces, nephews, brothers and sisters, fiancés, divorced spouses, and caregivers are sometimes mentioned in wills. Some even make provisions for their pets.

We have focused on who to give to financially for much of this chapter. But, as mentioned in Chapter 3, two types of legacies can positively affect our family trees and impact society. Footprints encapsulate tangible, physical resources like money, homes, properties, and cars. Heartprints are non-tangible assets like morals, family values, education, or family history. Let's talk about who may inherit those.

Giving away money is easier than passing down values. Descendants must buy into the principle for it to be transported into the next generation. For example, if you want your bloodline to continue your commitment to Christianity, your child has to share the same belief system. Without it, your faith legacy will not make it past your child's lineage. For your faith legacy to stay relevant through the years, each generation will have to commit to its importance. Because concepts are more challenging to pass on, you may have to plan for a heartprint differently than a footprint.

A footprint with a finite dollar amount attached will have a closed network of heirs. You may limit it to just your immediate family

---

43 Taylor, Chris. "70% of Rich Families Lose Their Wealth by the Second Generation." Money, June 17, 2015. https://money.com/rich-families-lose-wealth.

because adding too many people to the bank account will lessen the amount each person receives, diminishing the impact it could have on each person's life. A heartprint, however, may require the opposite. A larger volume of heirs gives the legacy a better chance of surviving. Because most heartprints are intangible, they can have infinite exposure without losing impact. They can be extended beyond your immediate family. Your children, parents, aunt, uncles, nieces, nephews, first, second, and third cousins, and community can be a part of your heartprint legacy plan.

Each year, my father's side of the family gathers for a reunion in east Texas at the Bluiett's Center. Members of the Bluiett family built the place to provide a comfortable, safe, and consistent place for the family to meet. The structure will last generations, symbolizing the Bluiett family heritage of love and commitment to each other. Think about the heartprints you would like to leave others, then consider the most reliable person to carry your legacy into the future.

Let's say you would like to create a digital family history book that includes names and pictures of your ancestors, their lineage, where they were born, and the type of occupation or community service they were involved in. Each year, it would need to be updated and reprinted to keep the book current and relevant for future kin. Who would be the best family member to do this? After talking to the clan, you find more than one person could fit the bill: your niece and a few cousins. Pull them all into your legacy plan and devise ways to update and hand the book down to the next generations.

Imagine you want to develop a family crest encompassing all the values your familial tribe stands for. When you mention this to your relatives, they love the idea. In fact, the artist in the family wants to design the crest, an elder wants to be a part of creating the value symbolism, and a business owner wants to print the family signage on shirts, socks, and bags. Give everyone interested a stake in creating the family logo to create alignment. Once the crest is complete, devise a communication plan to make sure everyone knows about it, understands its symbolism, and discusses ways to pass it on to future lineage. This is an example of getting unlimited family members involved in your legacy plan, likely ensuring its immortality.

When identifying heartprint goals, pen your thoughts on paper (or an electronic document) to keep your plan organized. Using the guidelines from Chapter 15, include these four essentials:

1. Make sure your goals are measurable.
2. Include the *why* behind your objectives.
3. List tactics/steps.
4. Provide time parameters.

Feel free to add additional components if it's helpful. For instance, the following table also includes participants.

Heartprint	Participants	Result	Timeline	Heirs
(*Specific*) Family college scholarships	All descendants of Mary Bluiett	(*Measurable*) $5,000 scholar fund	(*Time-bound*) - Donation due Dec. 31 of each year. - Grants given 1st quarter of each year.	(*Why*) All college-bound students in the family

Post your heartprint goals in a visible place so you can see them often. If you are like me, the out-of-sight, out-of-mind rule applies. Keeping goals in sight means I will always remember them. Share goals with your family or friends, especially if they are part of the project so that it will be top of mind for them, too. With some careful thought and a little work upfront, the recipients of your heartprints and footprints will be prepared to invest assets wisely and pass on family assets to many future generations.

Chapter 19:
Course Correction

When life throws curve balls, step back, adjust to your target, and then swing for the stands.

It only takes a second for plans you've carefully crafted to be wiped out or turned upside down. It's just the way things happen sometimes. Life is unpredictable, no matter how careful you are. While you can't control the unknown, you *can* manage how you react. And therein lies the key to success! According to Reliable Plant, only 20 percent of people set goals for themselves, which means that 80 percent of people *don't*. Even more unfortunate is that out of the 20 percent of people who set goals, only about 30 percent succeed. That means that only a third of those who set goals actually achieve them—6 percent of the goal-setters. That's pretty low odds. Having a goal and a plan is only half the battle to reach a vision. Being able to bounce back from a setback is the other half.

I had a friend who was in the process of sharing her life story in a publication called *Bounce-Back Ability*. Before she even started writing the book, she had already chosen the title because she understood the importance of getting back up, no matter how many times she was knocked down. This friend was diagnosed with cancer in her 30s. After treatment and strong determination, she became a cancer survivor. She vowed not to allow her illness to hold her captive and took her survival story on the road, speaking to audiences about her drive to overcome. Unfortunately, as she was writing her memoir in her early 40s, the cancer returned and stole her future. While this was a diagnosis she would not bounce back from, she planted a seed in me and many around her. When I think of her, I'm reminded that when hurdles suddenly appear, instead of stopping, I must find ways to jump them, go around them, or destroy them. Whatever it takes, we must find a way to keep moving forward. We may need to tap into our bounce-back ability when working toward a goal for several reasons. Some could be attributed to choices we've made; others may be entirely out of our control. Despite the issue, pivoting and moving forward is essential to reach victory.

Life Hack[44] cites the 11 most common reasons we may need to course correct.

1. Shifting Focus from Reward to Effort

Before starting the project, zoom in on the reward. However, when the hard work starts, focus more on the effort it takes to get that reward. To course correct—redirect your focus back to the reward and push through.

2. Goals Are Undefined or Unrealistic

Writing a bestselling novel is unrealistic if you rarely read a book or can't concentrate long enough to pen a paragraph. To course correct—choose something you can see yourself realistically doing. You will be motivated when you are inspired and feel a sense of purpose.

---

44   Porteous, Christ. "11 Reasons Why We Fail to Achieve Our Goals." Grey Smoke Media, August 10, 2023. https://www.lifehack.org/880259/why-we-fail-to-achieve-our-goals.

3. There Are Too Many Things on Your Plate
You may be spinning too many plates if you never complete a task or can't choose a priority. You have a finite amount of time and can't stuff everything into a day. To course correct—set some rules for yourself. Do not allow yourself to start another assignment until one is finished.

4. Poor Planning Derails All Efforts
If you half-heartedly think through steps from point A to point B, you will never reach point B. To course correct—take some time to strategize. Write it and follow the steps.

5. Losing Sight of the "Why" Factor
Identifying a goal is more productive when you understand the higher purpose. It's easy to give up once the initial excitement wears off when it's not connected to your "why." To course correct—know why your goal is relevant to encourage you to keep moving forward, even when the going gets tough.

6. Excuses, Excuses, and More Excuses
Things will go wrong. You can count on that. It's a part of life. When the inevitable happens, who do you blame? Excuses are convenient when dropping a goal, but they can also have a paralyzing effect. Excuses, if they run rampant, can derail everything you attempt. To course correct—take responsibility. Then, be resourceful, take control, and hit that goal.

7. Fear of Failure
Is the thought of failure holding you back? Focusing on failure can become crippling. But, there is a way to maneuver around the insecurity. To course correct—take some time to figure out what is causing the

fear. Then, retrain that voice in your head. You will learn to overcome what's mentally holding you back and charge forward to your goal.

8. Failing to Anticipate Obstacles

A perfectly planned plan is not going to go perfectly. Having a solid plan A is always good, but a great plan B isn't a bad idea either. To course correct, keep an agile mindset and anticipate a need for flexibility. Be ready to pivot to plan B if circumstances require the need.

9. There Is No Set Deadline

You are 42 percent more likely to achieve your goals if you write them down, but even then, if you don't have a deadline, they are typically not going to happen. To course correct—set a deadline for your goal. A deadline is essential to accomplishing a goal. It holds you accountable for your time.

10. Allowing Naysayers to Doubt the Goal

The bigger the vision, the more people you'll have doubting that you can accomplish it. To course correct—don't listen to naysayers. If you can't help it, use their judgment to fuel the fire and forge ahead. You've heard the saying, "Let your haters be your congratulators."

11. Procrastination Delays Goals

None of the reasons we fail to achieve our goals are as deadly as putting things off until tomorrow. We are all guilty of telling ourselves we will start tomorrow. Too many times, though, later never comes. Check out what the *Harvard Business Review* recommends to course correct—one of the best ways to beat procrastination is to commit publicly. Most people want to avoid looking lazy or like a failure.

If we look specifically at legacy goals and challenges that could hinder us from creating our desired outcomes, a few scenarios could throw us off track. What if we lose or have to recommit our finances and cannot transfer the wealth we initially projected? What do we do then? What if the person to whom we were hoping to grant property cannot receive it for one reason or another? What is next? What if our ancestor's heirloom pictures and audio stories were somehow destroyed, and we can't pass them on to loved ones? How do we make up for this?

These seem like devastating predicaments, but there are always opportunities to recover. If you lose your money, you could increase your life insurance to leave a more significant financial inheritance or pivot to the other type of legacy, heartprint. If giving to a particular family member doesn't make sense, give to another. Or find a special cause that will benefit people in the community. If you lose precious family keepsakes, like vintage photos or voice recordings, see if you can unearth photos from court records or archives from the library. Write down those precious stories before they are forgotten or re-record them in your voice to develop a new heirloom with historical significance to leave for future generations.

Whatever the complication, rework your plan to accomplish your goal of leaving a positive legacy. It may look different, but it could provide the same level of impact. Don't get hung up on what could have or should have happened. Course correct. Acknowledge the loss, then start thinking forward. Turn your sight and energy to what's in your control.

Unfortunate things can happen anytime; that's why it's so satisfying when things go as planned. But when conditions are not ideal, commit to pushing through obstacles and course correct as often as possible to reach your destination.

Part 6
Innovate

Innovation: Imagine the future and fill in the gaps.

—Brian Halligan, *CEO and cofounder Hubspot*

Chapter 20:
Digital Assets

What happens to our contacts, pictures, apps, social media, and other intellectual properties on our phones and laptops when we are no longer here? Good question, right?! Even if we are on top of our legacy game, we may not have considered our digital holdings.

As technology dominates our everyday lives, we should scrutinize how our digital assets will be handled with our passing. If we ignore this part of our possessions, we could put our family members in compromising positions while mourning our deaths.

To keep up with the dynamic cybernated marketplace, tech businesses have acknowledged digital legacies by creating legacy controls. Companies like Apple allow legacy contacts to be officially responsible for our electronic properties. A legacy contact is a person you choose to manage your accounts after you've passed away. Once you pass, your legacy contact gains access to certain parts of your account and can decide what happens to it and its content.

Everplans, an online company offering life organization and estate planning, provides a list of digital properties that may be helpful as you determine whether your online life needs an estate executor. You may be surprised at how much there is to take into account. Below are the three main categories and their descriptions (with some items in multiple categories):

Personal Digital Property

- Computing hardware, such as computers, external hard drives or flash drives, tablets, smartphones, digital music players, e-readers, digital cameras, and other digital devices
- Any information or data that is stored electronically, whether stored online, in the cloud, or on a physical device
- Any online accounts, such as email and communications accounts, social media accounts, shopping accounts, photo and video sharing accounts, video gaming accounts, online storage accounts, and websites and blogs that you may manage
- Domain names
- Intellectual property, including copyrighted materials, trademarks, and any code you may have written and own

Personal Digital Property with Monetary Value

- Computing hardware, such as computers, external hard drives or flash drives, tablets, smartphones, digital music players, e-readers, digital cameras, and other digital devices of monetary value
- Websites or blogs that generate revenue for you
- Art, photos, music, eBooks, intellectual property, or other digital property that generates revenue for you
- Accounts that are used to manage money and may hold money or credits, like PayPal, bank accounts, loyalty rewards programs, and any accounts with credit balances in your favor
- Domain names

Digital Business Property

- Any digital property owned by a business organization
- Any online accounts registered to the business

- Any assets of an online store you manage, such as your own online store or an eBay, Etsy, or Amazon store through which you sell things
- Any mailing lists, newsletter subscription lists, or email lists containing your company's clients
- Any client information, including customer history

Hardware and its contents could qualify as digital property depending on whether they contain information about you or items you have created—the same is true for your electronically stored data that could be housed in the cloud.

Some popular apps and services also include a legacy contact feature to help you plan for the future. Having legacy access to your account doesn't necessarily mean passing along all your logins and passwords, although that is not a bad idea. Legacy contacts cannot log into your account and see personal information; they can manage your settings, like who can post to your page and publish messages like memorial services or provide updates.

While there is no industry standard to how legacy controls work, many tech companies are catching on that this type of feature is needed.

The Washington Post suggests you consider the following important details when implementing a digital legacy:[45]

- Only add someone you trust—someone who knows and respects your wishes.
- Every couple of years, revisit the settings in case of changes, like a death, divorce, or a close friendship that has dissolved.

---

45   Kelly, Heather. "Your Data and Privacy." *The Washington Post*, March 20, 2022. https://www.washingtonpost.com/personal-tech/data-privacy.

- Review specifically what your legacy contact will have access to, as some kinds of data, like emails or direct messages, could feel too personal.
- Think about a backup plan for those accounts that do not have legacy options, like providing access to a password manager.
- Ensure your legacy contacts know you have chosen them to be the contact.
- If you have a will, consider including legacy contact documentation.

Contact the associated help desk to inquire how to set up legacy contacts or look for instructions on a search engine. Trust & Will, an online service that provides legal forms and information, advises adding digital assets to estate planning. Legacy contacts are just part of a contingency plan, states Trust & Will. You should include a detailed roadmap of handling online accounts and electronic property so the executor of your estate or beneficiary of your accounts can take control, fulfilling any last-minute wishes. In addition, Facebook removes pages memorialized and managed by a sole administrator. A second administrator would allow family to save the page and access pictures and other memories if you choose.[46]

---

46 "Estate Planning - Create an Online Will and Trust." Trust & Will. Accessed October 6, 2023. https://trustandwill.com.

Chapter 21:
Creative Gifts

You most likely have an idea of what types of gifts you would like to leave your family and the rest of society. However, I encourage you to review additional heartprints that could hold some intergenerational stamina. If you are looking for additional ways to impact your bloodline positively or have decided to leave an inheritance but do not know what to do, these ideas could be a perfect match or at least get your creative juices salivating. Before you start on a new heartprint, do a little snooping to uncover family projects that have gotten started and never finished for one reason or another. It may be your calling to complete them. Also, poll your elders to hear what they believe is needed. They are the minds of the past and eyes of the present. They may have the greatest idea and need someone younger to carry it out. Plus, your partnership could lead to a meaningful bonding period with your ancestors.

If you are starting from scratch, I have collected several ideas below, including win-win projects. Win-wins benefit you as well as your heirs. They could give you a better appreciation of your heritage and build a repository of historical family knowledge your descendants could learn from and add to for years. The proposals are separated into four categories of interest for ease of reading.

Win-Win Projects
- ***Research your family lineage and organize it into a book that can be passed down and added to through the generations***—A host

of online publishing websites can print your masterpiece. Create several copies to pass around to your family. Also, save your manuscript to pass along to trusted family members so they can easily add to the book.

- *Start a new tradition with your family*—Research meaningful family traditions and implement one your family will appreciate and want to carry forward. Be sure to explain why you are introducing a new family activity and stress the benefits for the family to gain buy-in.
- *Initiate your own business and involve family*—You could have large aspirations or smaller sentimental ones, but forming a business involving your family could keep them close, bonded, and teach them vital life skills for years. Did Grandma pass down her favorite candy recipe? Recreate the goodies, package them up, and sell them as a family. Did Grandpa purchase the necessary tools to create fancy walking canes? Use his tools to copy his designs and get the family involved in manufacturing and marketing them. Have fun while building something that could provide a livelihood to your loved ones.
- *Create a book of the family's favorite recipes*—Gather everyone's favorite recipes and organize them into a book. Cook each recipe with the family to get pictures of the food, with the family sitting around the table and enjoying the meal together.

Lineage Legacies

- *Keep a giving journal*—Record what you're giving and how it has impacted others. Whether it is money, time, or knowledge and wisdom, write the details and place it among other items you plan to leave for loved ones.

- *Start a photo journal*—Create a photo journal with descriptions, funny phrases the children said, dates and times of your life and family.
- *Design a family crest representing your family values*—Uncover your family's collective core values and design those principles into a family crest. Get everyone to participate to ensure an accurate representation and agreement. Have a family meeting to explain what the crest symbolizes and provide items with the new symbol embossed. Make sure you give all family members access to the crest with a few family rules of appropriate use.
- *Write Legacy Letters*[47]—Get some classic stationery and handwrite letters to your loved ones. A letter doesn't have to be long, but there's no limit. Be sure to include the most important elements, like what you want them to know about you, wisdom or life advice you want to pass on, and how much you love and care about them. Address the letters to each individual once you have composed them. Then, place them with your important documents. Let your loved ones know they are there.
- *Publish a collection of short stories or essays*—If you've heard an interesting tale from your elders, consider writing it down. True or false, funny or mysterious, it gives the younger generation a glimpse into the personalities of their ancestors.
- *Make a Legacy Quilt*[48]—Ask your family members to donate material, like an old basketball jersey, a first baby blanket, a tourist t-shirt from your visit to the Bahamas, or a commemorative tee from the 5k you ran together. Stitch it all together into a

---

47   Szczesniak, Daniel. "10 Meaningful Legacy Project Ideas." USUrns Online, April 30, 2019. https://www.usurnsonline.com/creative-ideas/10-meaningful-legacy-project-ideas.
48   Ibid.

tapestry that represents your lives. It will be a comforting legacy that goes beyond mere words.
- If you have a skill or craft, make something to leave behind, especially for your descendants.
- **Create a Legacy Box**[49]—Create something physical to pass on to those closest to you, like a keepsake box. You can fill it with notes, photos, and keepsakes or write a simple message and allow them to fill it with their own treasures.
- *Audio or Video recording*[50]—With smartphones, creating an audio or video recording is easier than ever. For audio, download an app and start talking. Some people find this much easier to do than to write, and your family will benefit from hearing your words in your voice. If you are recording a legacy video, it's probably better to write an outline of what you would like to say and practice your delivery before recording. Your loved ones will appreciate seeing your face and hearing your voice as you tell them you love them.

Celebrating Community Legacies

- *Take a youngster under your wing*—Become a mentor to someone in the community. Become a Big Brother or Big Sister or volunteer at a local school.
- **Start a new community program or greatly improve one that already exists**—Look for opportunities to improve your community. If you notice a need, find ways to take care of it. For instance, there may be a particular stretch of road that is always littered. Establish a group to keep it clean or join it if one already exists.

---

49   Ibid.
50   Ibid.

- *Raise funds to create a play area or improve a park in your neighborhood*—There can never be enough parks or playgrounds. There is something about a place of fun and respite that brings serenity to a neighborhood.
- *Start a new Bible study group for members of your community*—A community Bible study is a great way to bring neighbors together, setting the tone for brotherly love. Set up successors so the Bible study will live on once you retire.
- *Start an awards program*—Acknowledge community leaders and advocates for doing positive things in the city. Ceremoniously announce the recipients at an event, city council meeting, or on social media. Get local businesses to donate trophies or awards.
- *Be a connector*—Get to know the interests of people in the community and connect them with people of similar interests. You can help people with like minds become good friends. As a facilitator, you have the potential to link two or more people with life-changing ideas who need to find each other to produce something extraordinary.

Philanthropic Legacies

- *Start a family foundation*[51]—Establish a family foundation to provide financial grants for the community. Most family foundations are run by family members who voluntarily serve as trustees or directors. In many cases, the original donors' second- and third-generation descendants manage the foundation. In 2011, family foundations gave away approximately $21.3 billion in grants.

---

51   Ibid.

- ***Start a separate savings account and accumulate funds to provide an annual scholarship***—Put a small percentage of your wages into it and earmark it for scholarship or foundation donations. Find a high-yielding interest rate savings account and sock away funds to offer scholarships to family or community students. Even $1,000 could help a student buy books and other essentials for higher learning.
- ***Host a yearly fundraiser in your family's name to provide financial support to a worthy cause***—Get your family involved in holding an event that could raise funds for a worthy cause. Have fun with it. Create a theme and encourage community engagement with auctions, bingo, or a fun run. Get creative. Find sponsors to provide prizes. Be sure to invite the organization you donate to, as they can help drum up support.

Whether you choose one of the ideas above or have uncovered a unique opportunity, your passion will leave a heartfelt mark on your family and possibly the rest of the world.

Part 7
Economics

If you would not be forgotten as soon as you are dead, either write something worth reading or do something worth writing.

—Benjamin Franklin, *inventor*

Chapter 22:
The Numbers

I'm dedicating this entire section to economics because when I talk to people, this is the most delicate or misunderstood portion of inheritance. We are more comfortable leaving stories and family photos than finances and land. But building your family with assets is just as important as elevating your family with solid ethics, morals, history, and pride. We must teach ourselves and future generations to have a healthy relationship with money and discuss the importance of managing our currency while we are here and when we are gone.

Accumulated data from the Organization for Economic Cooperation and Development shows that inherited wealth in the U.S. has accounted for roughly 50 to 60 percent of private wealth since the early 1900s. What does this data tell us? Many families who figured out how to pass on and protect their family assets more than 100 years ago still have their wealth today. The heirs are still enjoying the fruits of their ancestor's labor. Passing wealth from generation to generation doesn't just happen. It takes planning. Providing financial gifts is just half the equation to a legacy of financial independence; the other half is teaching family how to preserve wealth for future generations.

Over the next 25 years, according to consulting group Cerulli Associates, an estimated $68 trillion will be transferred from U.S. households to heirs and charities. Without an estate plan or will, the assets that may have been intended for you could get tangled up in probate court. The cost of probate could be 3 to 8 percent of the value of an estate.[52] That's giving a hefty chunk of change your family worked hard for to the government if there's no will in place.

Let's use an inheritance of $100,000 as an example. An uncle passes away and leaves you and four of your cousins an inheritance of $100,000 to be split five ways: $20,000 for each person. But the commitment was only verbal. Your uncle told you and the other cousins that's how he wanted his money divided. He never wrote it in a will. Because there is no official document detailing your uncle's wishes, the government will hold onto the funds until a probate court rules in favor of you and your cousins. This will not only delay funds until the court makes a decision, but you may only receive $18,400 due to probate fees, throwing away up to $8,000. And that's the best scenario in this situation. What if another cousin contests your court petition? This would delay the payments even more and increase court fees and possible attorney fees. Your $20,000 inheritance could be shaved down to nothing.

A Consumer Report (CR) survey found that only one in three Americans say they have a will. The numbers are more staggering, comparatively speaking, between white and non-white U.S. citizens. Consumer Reports Nationally Representative Survey asked 2,224 people about wills and estate planning in April 2022. Sixty-one percent of whites and 67 percent of English-speaking Asians don't have a will. In comparison, CR found that 77 percent of Black people and 82 percent of Hispanic people do not have a will. "Those without a will cited several reasons, including the assumption that they don't have enough assets (25 percent overall), they're not sure how to create one (20 percent), they want their next of kin to receive everything automatically (9 percent), they think they're too young (23 percent),

---

52   "Invest in You: Ready. Set. Grow." CNBC, March 14, 2023. https://www.cnbc.com/invest-in-you.

or they just don't want to think about death (12 percent)." The most commonly selected reason among those without a will was that they plan to but haven't gotten around to it yet (43 percent).[53] Regardless of the reason, it's vital that you have a will, even if you have few assets or you're young. That way, you can make sure everything you own gets to the people you want to have it.

Here's a reality check for those without a will, believing their assets will automatically transfer to their next of kin. Your finances may still get tied up in the probate process, especially if you don't have your relatives' names on your banking accounts or list them as beneficiaries of your life insurance. When someone dies without a will, their state law will determine where assets go. A will can ensure that anything you own gets passed on precisely as you want, not as the state thinks you would want.

I imagine your thinking that this is common sense for the older generation. The ages of the adults surveyed by Consumer Report must have been young, right? Surprisingly, studies show that even people close to retirement lack a will. Just 55 percent of the survey respondents age 55 and older have a will. A mere 18 percent have what Bank of America Merrill Lynch calls the three essential documents for legacy planning: a will, a healthcare directive (specifying end-of-life preferences and designating someone to make health decisions for you if you can't), and a durable power of attorney (selecting someone to make financial and legacy-related decisions for you if you can't). Whether you are 18 or 55, a will should be the foundation of your financial legacy; construct the rest from there with a healthcare directive and power

---

53   Chang-Cook, Althea."Why People of Color Are Less Likely to Have a Will." Consumer Reports, August 10, 2022. https://www.consumerreports.org/money/estate-planning/why-people-of-color-are-less-likely-to-have-a-will-a6742820557.

of attorney. Several websites offer free templates to get you started or consult an expert.

Furthermore, willing your assets to your family, regardless of the amount, can be the lifeline your lineage needs to start on a path to financial stability. My grandfather inherited 22 acres from his father in Jasper County, Texas, in the mid-1900s. Back then, owning your own land was such an honor and a rarity in the Black community because so few held deeds. Land was the symbol of security as it provided a means to grow fruit and vegetables, raise cattle for meat or profit, and space to earn extra income by renting a portion of the property. Grandpa Charles Westmoreland Bluiett started his family on his inheritance in a small home the community helped to build. In 1946, Grandpa saved enough money from his logging job to hire a carpenter to build a larger dwelling for his growing household. Over time, he and Grandma Lodie Bell bought more than 100 additional acres surrounding the 22 passed down to Grandpa. As a child, I remember a vast farm that produced fields of green beans, peas, corn, okra, tomatoes, and peppers. There were trees loaded with pecans, persimmons, and pears. Horses, cows, and a mean old bull greeted us when we visited. During the summers and some holidays, my aunts, uncles, and cousins would gather on the front lawn to barbeque, grill hot dogs and hamburgers, and drink beer. The first time I drove a vehicle was a pickup truck around the boundless Bluiett farm. The huge plot of land holds footprints and heartprints, jewels our family will forever treasure.

My paternal grandparents wanted to make sure the legacy they built stayed within their genealogical unit. They developed an estate plan that divided the property equally among their direct descendants, each acquiring about 17 acres. Today, all of the acreage is still in the hands of the Bluiett family. The remaining siblings live in big cities now. They may sell timber occasionally, but the homestead is a place of rest and relaxation and is available if family members need it. The inherited land Grandpa received allowed him to provide a better life for his family, giving my dad and his siblings a spacious place to grow and thrive. Grandpa Bluiett was a glowing example of legacy living, and we are beyond blessed for the intergenerational boost he bestowed upon our family.

Money experts say start at home if you want to build wealth to pass on to future generations.

Commit to your children's financial education. Raising financially responsible and independent adults is critical to creating lasting wealth. Help your children understand checks and balances to enable them to support themselves. Start having honest conversations about money at home at an early age so your kids know they can ask questions. Suggested topics include need versus want, how to earn money, savings, and the importance of giving back. Have fun with financial literacy quizzes. As kids age, introduce them to more advanced personal finance concepts like banking and investing. The goal is that they are equipped to be financially responsible when they leave the house as young adults. This can be intimidating, especially when figuring out your own finances. But, most people learn more from their failures than their successes, especially regarding money. Our children can benefit from our financial wins, and they can also learn from our financial mistakes. We should not hide our money failures and what we did wrong. Sharing our losses and what we learned from them can help our children avoid some of the mistakes we made.

Another tip to build wealth is to invest in the stock market. Dabbling in the stock market allows you to build passive income and protect your money from inflation. Most people who invest in the stock market with a long-term plan and diversify their portfolios generally increase their assets over time. The S&P 500, an index that tracks the stock of 500 of the largest U.S. companies, has returned 10 percent on average before inflation since 1926.[54] As a beginner, a simple way to get started is through low-cost index funds, which provide long-term growth opportunities at relatively low fees. Consider signing up for free banking tools to analyze your investments easily.

Real estate investment is also helpful in building wealth. Real estate usually appreciates over time and can render cash flow opportunities. Some investors start by moving out of their homes, renting them out, and purchasing another property. This allows you to build your real estate portfolio one house at a time.

If you possess business savvy, create a company to pass down to your children. More than 30 percent of family-owned businesses are second-generation, according to Conway Center for Family Business. Ensure your kids work in the establishment at a young age so they are comfortable with the inner workings. This will encourage them to take over once you retire. But if your children are not interested in taking the helm, there is still a potential to create wealth by selling the business.[55]

---

54   Wealth, Anne-Lyse. "Generational Wealth: What It Is & How to Build It." Empower, January 31, 2023. https://empower.com/the-currency/money/how-to-build-generational-wealth.
55   Ibid.

Chapter 23:
How to Leave a Financial Gift

Everyone can leave a monetary gift to a loved one, even if you don't think you have much to give. There are different ways you can plan for your family's financial future. This chapter explores estate planning tools like life insurance, Last Will and Testaments, trusts, and living wills.

Life Insurance

If you don't have life insurance, you need to get it. Life insurance is one of the easiest ways to leave a financial windfall to your heirs. Life insurance provides financial protection, among other benefits, for your family when you pass away. Many of us leave the earth without considering the financial burden of a simple funeral. Burials are expensive. If your loved ones are forced to pay for your funeral, your death could develop a financial hardship for them. You can avoid this if you acquire life insurance. You can make monthly payments on a death payout that could finance your burial and leave additional funding to help your loved ones.

Not quite sure how life insurance works? You're not alone. "Only 31 percent of Americans feel knowledgeable about life insurance," stated the Life Insurance Market Research Association. That means almost 70 percentof Americans are clueless. There are two types of life insurance: Term Life and Whole or Permanent Life Insurance. Term Life policies last for a set amount of time, and then expire. Term Life is less expensive than whole life insurance and is usually acquired during an adult's working years. It could provide for a family if a significant salary is taken away due to someone's death.

Whole or permanent life insurance does not expire. It costs more than Term Life, however, but ensures a payout whenever the insured passes away, regardless of age. Many money experts recommend investing in life insurance if you want to leave your family a financial gift. It is vital for a young family with children that would lose essential income with your passing. The funds your family receives from life insurance could pay your family's bills like house notes, car payments, and college tuition, which is helpful as your spouse finds financial footing.

Although women make up more than half of the American workforce[56], we are less likely than men to have life insurance. Roughly six in ten men own life insurance, while women represent less than one in five. In fact, life insurance ownership by women has been on the decline for the past five years in a row.[57] If you do not hold life insurance and have decided to purchase a policy, here are a few things to consider when choosing the best coverage for you and your family:

- How much life insurance do you need? Look at how much money your family would need to continue their same lifestyle if you passed away (considering mortgage, property taxes, utilities, cars, food, babysitters, college for kids, etc.). Financial calculators on life insurance websites help you determine how much you need.

---

56   "Women in the Workforce Statistics 2023: Roles and Pay Gap." TeamStage, March 14, 2023. https://teamstage.io/women-in-the-workforce-statistics.
57   Crail, Chauncey. "Life Insurance Statistics, Data and Industry Trends 2023." Forbes, June 21, 2023. https://www.forbes.com/advisor/life-insurance/life-insurance-statistics.

- Many jobs offer life insurance as a benefit. Look at the potential payout to determine if that would be enough funds to support your family. If it's not enough, you can also add supplemental life insurance for a monthly fee to make up the difference through your job. You could also invest in an individual policy outside of your job.
- Go to a licensed broker for private life insurance: a financial advisor (they already know your financial picture), an independent broker, an affiliated agent, or a digital life insurer.
- Reach out to friends and family for a recommended insurer. If you find an insurer online, make sure you read the reviews.
- The key is to do your research first and have an idea of what you want in the amount of coverage. Try finding a life insurance calculator online to access the amount needed for coverage.
- There will possibly be a medical probe to determine your health status. Many companies will not cover you if you are a smoker or have serious health issues. Some companies will consider other factors of your background outside your health, like your driving record, criminal and credit history, and bankruptcy.[58]

Last Will and Testaments

Think of a Last Will and Testament as a gift to your loved ones. A final expression of love that shows your heirs you wanted to take care of them to the best of your ability. Leave them everything of value that you can't take with you to your final resting place. It's also a chance to be clear about how you want your belongings organized and distributed. This can decrease worry and stress and be a form of solace as family members are grieving. The last thing they need is the heavy responsibility of figuring out your wishes or, even worse, facing a probate court.

---

58   Ibid.

If you do not leave a will, your possessions become the responsibility of the state you lived in. Your family will have to appeal the court to gain ownership of your belongings, a costly and sometimes contentious event. So do your family a favor and leave a will.

Remember, wills are legal documents. If yours could get complicated or will likely be contested or challenged, seek legal advice. Heirs (family members), beneficiaries (anyone named in the will), and creditors can contest or challenge your will.[59] If you decide not to include your spouse or immediate family members or know family members will believe your will is unfair, consult an expert. There are various clauses to include in your will to keep it just how you want it. However, if you don't anticipate any issues, you can download a free template from a reputable website online. Be sure to google templates from your state to keep you within the guidelines of your local laws. Each state has nuances that may require different actions, like having a witness to the will or notarizing the document to ensure your will is valid.

Finally, make sure you have a trusted individual (child, family friend, attorney) to carry out your wishes as executor of the will. Don't hide your will, but ensure it's in a safe, protected place and keep it updated.

Living or Family Trust

A trust manages, controls, and passes on assets such as investments, property, and cash.[60]

A living or family trust may be beneficial in managing family assets after you have passed away. To set up a trust fund, three entities

---

59 Joseph Fawbush, Esq. FindLaw. Accessed October 6, 2023. https://www.findlaw.com/company/our-team/joseph-fawbush-esq.
60 "Your Local Solicitors, Leaving You with One Less Worry." GloverPriest Solicitors - Personal & Business Lawyers. Accessed October 6, 2023. https://gloverpriest.com/.

are required: the grantor, the person(s) who provides the assets for the trust; the beneficiary, the person(s) who receive assets from the trust; and the trustee, the person(s) who manages the trust.

The main difference between a living and a family trust is that a living trust can distribute assets to anyone named as a beneficiary when the person who set up the trust dies. Beneficiaries can include any person or thing like family, friends, charities, alma maters, and pets. Once the owner or the grantor passes away, the assets from the trust will be distributed according to the grantor's wishes. This is especially helpful if the grantor anticipates someone contesting the inheritance. It protects the assets from probate.

A family trust, however, is designed to benefit only the family members of the person who set up the trust. A family trust can extend through generations and will have a trustee to manage assets and administrative duties.

There are advantages and disadvantages to setting up a trust, some of which are listed below. Do your homework and talk to a financial planning expert before diving in. First, let's look at some advantages:

Creditor Protection:

If assets are transferred to a trust before a settlement is required, creditors may be unable to access them because an individual debtor does not own the property. It belongs to a group of people within the trust.[61]

Community Property Protection:

If someone inherits assets within a family trust, unnamed spouses or partners will not have access to the properties. This is especially important in the case of divorce or a breakup.[62]

---

61   Pearse Trust, Inc, pearce-trust.ie.
62   Kiplinger.com, December 2022.

Family Members with Special Needs:
Family trusts can protect family members with special needs who cannot manage their assets. Instructions or guidelines can be set to limit use.[63]

Reckless Spending:
Long-term protection can be instated in a family trust, which offers more guidelines than handing a family member an inheritance without parameters. This is useful for family members who need to improve at managing their finances.[64]

Succession Planning:
Succession planning allows a retiring generation to pass family values and traditions to future generations with structured guidelines to keep the family trust in good standing and keep assets within the family.[65]

Estate Planning:
Upon the death of a family member who has assets within a trust, any debt of the deceased cannot be taken from the property within the trust. Therefore, protecting property within the family trust from creditors.[66]

Taxes:
For wealthy families, a trust could be a tax shelter. The federal estate tax ranges from 18 to 40 percent depending on the amount someone inherits. Wealthy families who inherit $12.92 million or more may avoid some or all of the estate taxes due when someone passes away if

---

63   Ibid.
64   Ibid.
65   Ibid.
66   Ibid.

assets are transferred to a living or family trust. Besides federal taxes, some states will levy an estate tax. Be sure to check laws for your state to determine if heirs are subject to additional taxes.[67]

The advantages sound very appealing. Make sure, however, to look at the whole picture. There are some disadvantages to consider as well.

Costs:

Setting up a family trust costs more than creating a will. You can consult an attorney or find a free template online to make a will. However, trusts require legal assistance and, thus, more expenses. In addition, a financial institute will probably administrate the trust, which means banking fees. Setting up a trust can cost up to $7,000, depending on the complexity, according to Smartassets.com. Also, consider the costs of drafting documents and transferring property.

No Individual Ownership:

When someone places assets in a trust, such as property, they no longer own that property personally. That asset is owned and managed by the trustees, the legal owners of the trust. This means you don't have the right to sell the property whenever you like unless you're the trustee. It must be an agreed transaction by the trustees.[68]

Administrative Responsibilities:

Trustees are responsible for managing the trust, which includes paying income taxes. Trustees must stay on top of tax laws or hire someone who does.[69]

---

67   Ibid.
68   Pearse Trust, Inc, pearce-trust.ie; Insigna Financial Ltd.
69   "Your Local Solicitors, Leaving You with One Less Worry." GloverPriest Solicitors - Personal & Business Lawyers. Accessed October 6, 2023. https://gloverpriest.com.

Remember, the key to creating a worry-free trust is checking out the small print and understanding the laws governing it. Consult a financial advisor before moving forward. If done correctly, a trust could offer many bonuses. On the other hand, if you try to establish one without help, you could face costly pitfalls.

Living Will

Don't forget about your living will—a living will administers guidance to loved ones and protection for yourself in times of medical crisis. It helps family members honor your medical wishes if you cannot speak for yourself. A living will directs healthcare providers on which medical and surgical treatments you would and would not like to have. Types of directives placed in a living will may include your preference for resuscitation, ventilators, breathing tubes, organ donations, and pain management.[70]

Another consideration is assigning a power of attorney for healthcare decisions. Living wills and powers of attorney partner to offer greater protection. Using a durable power of attorney form, you can designate someone to make healthcare decisions on your behalf if you are incapacitated. Just make sure the person you appoint is well aware of your wishes.

You can find free templates for living wills and medical power of attorney forms online. These can be used as a guide to create your own document. Some living wills require two witnesses, and others require notarization. Search for forms used in your state to keep you current on local criteria.

Once you complete your living will and power of attorney documents, ensure family members and important people know your

---

70   "Advance Directives." Johns Hopkins Medicine. Accessed October 6, 2023. https://www.hopkinsmedicine.org/all-childrens-hospital/patient-families/patient-family-resources/spiritual-care/advance-directives.

desires. Feel free to give a copy to your current healthcare provider in the event they are approached.

If you take advantage of the estate planning tools mentioned in this chapter, you are well on your way to providing your family with a financial gift. Don't get discouraged by the amount you think you can leave. Even a small contribution can enhance someone's life. It's more important to focus on making sure what you possess is legally assigned to a beneficiary once you pass away. The best financial gift you can give is stress-free and without legal entanglements.

Part 8
Share

My legacy is that I stayed on course ... from the beginning to the end because I believed in something inside of me.

—Tina Turner, *singer, entertainment icon*

Chapter 24:
Gather

Know your giving story.

Keep account of what you are giving, how much you are giving, and where you are giving. This is not for bragging rights. Being able to articulate your contributions to society has several benefits, and none of them, we will discuss, are selfish.

Documenting your donations of time, energy, and money can encourage you to stay motivated. Recounting what you have given has an empowering effect and usually stimulates good feelings, triggering you to give more. Generally, giving makes us happy, according to Charity Link, a blog about fundraising. We are hard-wired when it comes to pleasure—many people feel a rush of inner warmth and contentment when they donate. What's even more interesting, reports the blog, is we can train and activate our brain's reward circuit. If we have a particular set of beliefs, we can trigger a sense of pleasure by acting by those beliefs.

Let's take that a step further; if we believe that we must leave a positive legacy to society, our brains will send happy signals when we realize we are progressing toward our goal.[71] That cheerfulness could propel us to exceed our objectives because who would want to stop pushing that happy button? Keeping an account also helps us to know

---

71   Charity Link. "How Fundraisers Can Use the Psychology of Giving." Charity Link, February 22, 2023. https://www.charitylink.net/blog/how-fundraisers-can-use-psychology.

where we've been and how much further we need to go to reach our full legacy potential.

Another reason we should chronicle our benevolence is that it could provide a sense of pride and encouragement for our bloodline if we relay this information to them. Think about those who stand a little taller when talking about what their father passed along to the family or their mother gave to the community. Those charitable offerings feel like an extension of the descendants because the children are directly linked to their parent's bloodline. I get warm and fuzzy when people talk about how my parents inspired them. For instance, one of my younger cousins stood up at my mother's 70th birthday party and affectionately described how she watched my mother's life and wanted to be like her to the point of buying the same car. My mom represented determination, hard work, and success; my cousin wanted to emulate that. My father, as a Baptist minister, visited sick members of his church when they were immobile and could not make it to Sunday service. It's touching to hear those church-goers and their family members express how uplifting it was for my dad to appear by their bedside, at home or the hospital, to pray for them. It's humbling to know family members were servant leaders in the community. Knowing that our ancestors are responsible for enriching society in various ways carries rich appreciation that could incentivize many along our genealogical thread to keep the goodwill going. It's the gift that keeps giving as it offers double the rewards. The first reward is the actual material that is given to others. The second reward is the inspirational legacy proliferating generation after generation.

Your philanthropic ties could also influence others to give. Think about meeting someone passionate about the work they've done in the community and how that engagement triggers your passions, kindling an urge to find ways to uplift others. Sharing your giving philosophy could galvanize others to "pay it forward." According to experts, exchanging giving narratives can also produce sentiments of togetherness. It prompts feelings of being part of something much larger than ourselves, believing that participating in widespread benevolent movements could lead to favorable world change.

A study published in the *Proceedings of the National Academy of Science* by James Fowler of the University of California, San Diego, and Nicholas Christakis of Harvard shows that when one person behaves generously, it influences observers to act generously toward others as well. The researchers found that altruism could spread by three degrees, from person to person to person. As a result, Fowler and Christakis say that each person in a network can influence dozens or even hundreds of people, some of whom they've never met.[72] Volunteering your time, donating money, and providing other charitable resources are notable, but illustrating and articulating your giving to others multiplies the benefits. It could jumpstart a cascade of generosity throughout the community and the world.

Documenting your donations is the best way to ensure you are in touch with the sum of your contributions, and there are simple ways to do this. You could keep a running list of what you did, when, and who it went to. Write it down clearly in a journal or save it on your laptop. To provide a more comprehensive outline, I suggest also noting the focus of the impact. The reason you are giving or the results of your giving is even more significant than what you gave. Add "impact" to your list so anyone who reads it gets the whole picture. For instance, if you gave $1,000 to a fund that provides scholarships to students who otherwise would not be able to attend college, your log could look something like this:

---

72   Marsh, Jason, and Jill Suttie. "5 Ways Giving Is Good for You." Greater Good Magazine, 2010. https://greatergood.berkeley.edu/article/item/5_ways_giving_is_good_for_you.

Date	Given	Charity	Impact
August 1, 2023	Donated $1,000 to college fund	Texas College fund charities	This fund provided 15 scholarships to students from all over the state.

Adding the impact illustrates the need and the results of your giving. Quick bullet points do the trick. Once you have built your donation chest, your log will show how much, over time, you've contributed and the causes you are truly passionate about. If you have given to one charity more than others, your log will show this trend. It could help you uncover a passion you may not have recognized.

You may find you gave more than you realized. For instance, if you donated about $300 every three months for the past decade, you have racked up some giving mileage. Ten thousand dollars in 10 years is a big deal. You should feel both accomplished and inspired by this outcome. Or you could decide that you want to give more.

Also, keep track of the time you have given to the community. It's also a part of your story. If you volunteered 100 hours giving back to the community last year, write that down. Those hours add up; you could have 1,000 hours of community work before you know it. That's something worth celebrating and building on! Here's an example of how you could log your hours:

Date	Given	Charity	Impact
August 1 – 5, 2023	Volunteered 10 hours at the food back	Food Bank of Dallas Texas	Organized perishable inventory so food set to expire the earliest would be given out first, thus increasing fresh fund contribution about 5%

At the end of each year, you could add a field to your spreadsheet to add up totals like below:

Date	Given	Charity	Impact
August 1 – 5, 2023	Volunteered 10 hours at the food back	Food Bank of Dallas Texas	Organized perishable inventory so food set to expire the earliest would be given out first, thus increasing fresh food contribution to community about 5%
October 2023	Volunteered 15 hours at animal shelter	Houston Animal Shelter	Exercised the dogs, cleaned kennels at underfunded shelter

YEAR	TOTAL VOLUNTEER HOURS		
2023	25 hours	Food Bank Animal Shelter	1. Increased fresh food contributions by 5% 2. Enhanced underfunded shelter

Lastly, create a statement with the personal data you've collected to easily share your history during appropriate times. Here's an example using the data above: "*I am passionate about ensuring no one goes hungry. I believe everyone has the right to eat healthy foods. I volunteer at the food bank and donate other resources to ensure everyone in my community is fed.*" Or, "*I believe in advocating for the underdog, especially those who do not have a voice. That's why I volunteer at the local animal shelter. I want to make sure they have a clean, safe, and healthy environment.*"

Knowing what and where you have given helps you understand your humanitarian path. Seeing how far you've come with your objectives could motivate you. It could inspire your family and younger generations and spur a ripple effect of generosity throughout the community.

Chapter 25:
Share

Once you have figured out your giving story, take the next step and share it. Consider how you will relay those details to your family, friends, and the rest of the community. There are many ways to get the word out. Choosing the most appropriate method for a specific audience could be the key to whether your legacy is carried through many generations or stops at just one.

For instance, if you expect your generous history to be passed on to your children's children, you should not just rely on word of mouth. Our memories are faulty, and you would risk your accomplishments being altered or forgotten. You could, however, include your legacy in your will, which is considered a public record. Anyone searching court documents could find it. Make it easy for your descendants to get to know you, even long after you are gone, by adding details of your contributions in your will. You could also place your giving journal among your important papers. That way, your heirs will see the importance of your altruism as your log will be among your most vital records like your will, banking statements, deeds, stock accounts, bonds, etc.

If you are a professional and have a resume or CV (Curriculum Vitae) for interviewing or speaking engagements, make sure to incorporate your giving story into these documents to give your employers a better understanding of who you are and provide your audience with knowledge of your philanthropic commitment to the community. Your generosity will become a highlight in your career, broadening your legacy to a diverse group of people.

Here's an opportunity to get creative. Write your biography exclusively to pass on to future generations. Add pictures and special quotes to keep it interesting. It's easy to self-publish these days. Search for an inexpensive online company to help you with this, or find a printer with a template that allows you to drop in words and photos. I'm sure there are many unique ways to deliver your legacy to your successors.

Some people have contemplated the best words to describe or ask for donations. Certain expressions will turn people off. For instance, researchers advise against saying give or gave. Studyfinds.org published an article by John Anderer titled "Don't Say Give? Studies Find It Actually Hurts Charitable Donations." The post explains, "The word 'give' can have a more negative connotation than 'spend' to donors. 'Give' highlights how you're being separated from your money, which is not appealing," says study co-author Selin Malkoc, associate professor of marketing at Ohio State's Fisher College of Business. But "spend" your money or time has a different connotation. Potential donors feel they are still part of the cash and still in control of it. People who were asked for a financial donation offered more than twice as much when charities asked them to "spend" their money ($94) in comparison to asking them to "give" a donation ($40), according to Ohio State researchers.[73] This is something to consider when articulating your giving story. Some terms can be more energizing than others.

Whether you are spending or giving, ensuring your family and community are exposed to how you've given back to society has several benefits. Ego aside, it can build confidence in some and encourage others to follow in your footsteps. There is no better legacy than one that lives on in others.

---

73 Anderer, John. "Don't Say Give? Studies Find It Actually Hurts Charitable Donations." StudyFinds, April 14, 2022. https://studyfinds.org/dont-say-give-charitable-donations.

Chapter 26:
Give Thanks

Ground yourself with gratitude.

As you check off each objective leading to your mission, you should take time to rejoice. Celebrations are an act of gratitude. Celebrate those who supported you along the way, and praise the Ultimate Helper for allowing you to be a vessel of change. Give yourself credit for hanging in there until you complete your assignment. Take time to recall all the moments of hard work, the opportunities that just fell into your lap, the strength it took to keep moving forward, the money that materialized to fund your mission, the expert that appeared to bring your dream to the next level, and all the divine impressions that made your vision a success. Sometimes, when we accept a task, everything seems to fall into place. That is the harmonious alignment of God and humans moving in unison. Hallelujah! This is a reason to celebrate.

As the saying goes, find joy in the journey because you will spend more time there than in the moment you hit your goal. Once you meet your objectives, you'll start over again, striving to achieve something new. So take the time to show appreciation and gratefulness for each day you are granted to fight for something you believe in. Improving a community, being a source of hope, breaking familial chains, and disrupting negative generational patterns should be revered and acknowledged. Delight in the new traditions you helped to create and the milestones you have reached. Even if you don't see the fruits of your labor, when no root has breached the surface, trust that when you do the right thing, you are rewarded. Our faithfulness should allow our hearts to leap for joy.

Practicing gratitude tends to validate our sense of purpose and meaning in life. We are inspired to work harder toward our goals when we are grateful for opportunities, resources, and support. It can keep us motivated to continue giving back. Appreciation serves as positive reinforcement to encourage us to continue the behavior or action that led to the positive outcome. It energizes us to replicate that same behavior in the future. So, don't put off celebrating. Be grateful for each breakthrough.

Another way to show thanks is to take action. Legacy livers honor the future by stepping up today. Use this forward thinking to stand up and start walking towards your best you. Follow the call that leads to your purposeful life to reap your rewards sooner rather than later. It's not a coincidence that procrastination can lead to reduced satisfaction in life. It is the opposite of taking action. Procrastination causes stress, depression, anxiety, and fatigue, according to a life satisfaction study published in the National Institute of Health's National Library of Medicine.[74]

We feel devalued and left behind when we don't progress in life. But, when you force yourself to move forward, you feel accomplished and worthy. Show yourself appreciation by taking the leap to achieve something that makes you proud.

In earlier chapters, we discussed activities that positively affect our mental and physical health. Like giving to others and providing for our offspring, expressing gratitude is linked to increased happiness. It

---

74   Beutel, Manfred E., Eva M. Klein, Stefan Aufenanger, Elmar Brähler, Michael Dreier, Kai W. Müller, Oliver Quiring, et al. "Procrastination, Distress and Life Satisfaction across the Age Range – a German Representative Community Study." PLOS ONE 11, no. 2 (2016). https://doi.org/10.1371/journal.pone.0148054.

helps to shift our focus from negative thoughts to positive ones, leading to a more optimistic mindset. Research suggests gratitude can also have favorable consequences for us biologically. Thankful people may experience lower stress levels, improved sleep, and a stronger immune system.[75]

I'm grateful for the opportunity to share my passion for the importance of passing on a positive heritage. My goal with this book is to open dialogue among families and ignite movement toward living a legacy today that will enhance our children's lives tomorrow. Regardless of how old you are, if you are reading this, you can improve the people and circumstances around you. It simply takes a willingness to try, a plan, and a commitment.

Don't forget to give thanks and open your heart to receive thanks along the way. It is God's will that we lean on each other and share our talents and gifts with each other. He is waiting to give us all a heavenly high-five and say, "Well done, good and faithful servant! You have been faithful with a few things; I will put you in charge of many things. Come and share your master's happiness" (Matt. 25:23 NIV).

---

75   Logan, Amanda. "Can expressing gratitude improve your mental, physical health?" Mayo Clinic Health System, Dec. 6, 2022. https://www.mayoclinichealthsystem.org/hometown-health/speaking-of-health/can-expressing-gratitude-improve-health.

If you believe in the legacy concepts in this book, will you help me spread the word?

There are several ways you can help me get the word out about the message of this book …

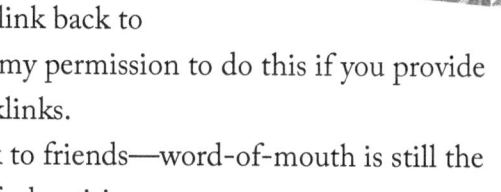

- Post a 5–Star review on Amazon.
- Write about the book on your Facebook, Twitter, Instagram, LinkedIn—any social media you regularly use!
- If you blog, consider referencing the book, or publishing an excerpt from the book with a link back to my website. You have my permission to do this if you provide proper credit and backlinks.
- Recommend the book to friends—word-of-mouth is still the most effective form of advertising.

You can reach me at: www.legacylivingwithtante.com

www.ingramcontent.com/pod-product-compliance
Lightning Source LLC
Chambersburg PA
CBHW070152100426
42743CB00013B/2892